Praise for
New Way to Be Hu

"Artists are the best theologians. They feel things that are true before theologians can jargonize them into obscurity. What Charlie Peacock has written in this book is a good example of theological truth stated in a way that only an artist can."

    —TONY CAMPOLO, PHD, professor emeritus of sociology,
      Eastern University

"*New Way to Be Human* is a 'just in time' book for me, speaking to many of the questions I have been wrestling with concerning how to actually live out this kingdom dream. This conversation about storied living is helping me expose and shed some of the subplots in my life that are incongruent with the larger story God is telling through his Word and work. Charlie inspires me to wake up each day to be a student-follower of Jesus Christ and nothing else."

    —SARA GROVES, recording artist and songwriter

"Charlie Peacock takes us from the prophets of Israel to the prophets of song and cinema. He leads us on a journey that passes loopy stories and scholarly citations. It answers questions that are so real, so direct, so heartfelt that you may not be sure whether you are having fun or becoming a more authentic disciple."

    —DAN DORIANI, author of *The Life of a God-Made Man*
      and Putting the Truth to Work

"Few people have the necessary gifts to communicate wonder in both music and words, and Charlie Peacock is one of those rare artists. In both the poetry of his lyrics and the thoughtful prose of his books, he asks just the right questions so that we can see more deeply. Those hungry to be fully human will gravitate to *New Way to Be Human* not because Charlie is clever (though he is), but because his heart and imagination are aflame with the Story that brings both grace and hope in our fragmented world."

—DENIS D. HAACK, Ransom Fellowship, editor of *Critique*

"This is a splendid book about real life in a good but fallen world where grace yet abounds. Peacock writes with compassion, integrity, and discernment."

—QUENTIN J. SCHULTZE, author of *Habits of the High-Tech Heart: Living Virtuously in the Information Age*

"This book will make you want to live. Not a tedious breathing in and out, in and out...but how you've known it should be. Your ideas about relationship with the Divine will expand."

—DAVID CROWDER, recording artist

"There is something very freeing in Charlie's words: 'You can still be a student-follower of Jesus and not possess all truth, once-for-all universal certainty, and the answer to every question.' Much of my experience with American Christianity has been like an overly simplistic tract that tries too hard and says too little. This book has inspired me to reread and retell the Story with 'the widest, clearest view.' In sharing the clues he has found along the way, Charlie reminds me that I must humbly embrace what I know for sure, yet hold myself open to the mystery of the bigger Story."

—CHRISTINE DENTE, songwriter and recording artist (Out of the Grey)

"I've known Charlie Peacock for twenty years as a songwriter, artist, and producer, but now he explodes on the scene as a deep-thinking theologian. Charlie has given this Wesleyan new insight on what it means to be fully sanctified. You will love *New Way to Be Human*."

—BARRY LANDIS, president of Word Label Group

New Way to Be Human

A Provocative Look
at What It Means to Follow Jesus

Charlie Peacock

Foreword by Jon Foreman

SHAW BOOKS
an imprint of WATERBROOK PRESS

New Way to Be Human
A SHAW BOOK
PUBLISHED BY WATERBROOK PRESS
2375 Telstar Drive, Suite 160
Colorado Springs, Colorado 80920
A division of Random House, Inc.

Many of the illustrations in this book reflect real names and stories and are used by permission. Names and details in a few stories have been changed to protect the identities of the persons involved.

ISBN 0-87788-071-9

Library of Congress Cataloging-in-Publication Data
Peacock, Charlie.
    New way to be human : a provocative look at what it means to follow Jesus / Charlie Peacock.—1st ed.
        p. cm.
    Includes bibliographical references.
    ISBN 0-87788-071-9
    1. Christian life. I. Title.
BV405.3.P43 2004
248.4—dc22   2003023045

Printed in the United States of America
2004—First Edition

10 9 8 7 6 5 4 3 2 1

To Alice Ashworth—
mother, friend, and sister in the Jesus Way.
Your encouragement has never wavered.
Bless you.

Contents

Making the New Way Visible

Foreword

I was nineteen years old, eating grapes in a San Diego music studio, wide-eyed. I'm pretty sure I was grinning. I had been looking forward to this moment for weeks: The head of an independent record label had flown all the way from Nashville to hear my friends and I play music—our music.

We were young. We were green. We had dreams that couldn't pay the rent. We threw every song that we knew down on tape and drove our new friend from the record label, Charlie Peacock, back to the airport.

No one has ever heard those tapes.

Because the airlines lost Charlie's luggage on his return flight, the recording session will forever be remembered in gracious approximations. And that, my friend, is probably one of the biggest reasons that we were signed.

There are no coincidences in this story (and I'm grinning again). Over the past seven years, I've all but overstayed my welcome at the Peacock house. Charlie Peacock has become like a second father to me—a mentor in life and love and melody. I've driven his car, eaten his ice cream, and fallen in love on his front porch with a girl who would become my wife. So many dreams, so many melodies. All along Charlie was patient, teaching me how to sing a song, how to live a life of poetry.

"New Way to be Human" was a song I wrote at Charlie's house during a really difficult time in my life. I was at the breaking point. I was numb to the trends and the hype; I didn't care about the facade anymore. I wanted to sing a song about real life, to sing about the only compelling reason to keep on living—or rather, to begin to live. You see, living is not a simple matter of breathing and talking and eating. Whoever tries to keep his life will lose it, and whoever loses his life will preserve it. Perhaps our compass was wrong all along: Maybe wealth, fame, and power do not bring happiness.

So in this upside-down age, we turn to the singers and the dreamers to bring us back to reality. The poets speak highly of my predecessors. They tell me that to be human is a noble thing, that my species, made in the image of God himself, is the crown of creation that has been given dominion over all the earth. With this in mind I wonder at times if I'm truly human. Sure, I have opposable thumbs and I walk erect. I vote and mow the lawn and eat fast food, but the "crown of creation?" Not sure about that one. The life I live could often be deemed the banality that is the existence of a twenty-first-century human. As Pascal wrote, "What a chimera, then, is man! What a novelty, what a monster, what a chaos, what a subject of contradiction, what a prodigy! A judge of all things, feeble worm of the earth, depositary of the truth, cloaca of uncertainty and error, the glory and the shame of the universe!"

I know that things should be otherwise. I know that simple "existence" is not to be equated with life—surely not! What a gift is breath! What a privilege to love and feel the pains and joys of youth. And even still, my life is so prone to mediocrity. I yearn to live and love and burn, and yet so much of my time is spent faking and forgetting, faking and forgetting.... I carry out my disbelief with uninspired hands, my eyes shut, my emotions dulled, my spirit numb. In times like these I am in desperate need of truth to come to me like a blinding light, like a splinter in my soul, reminding me of the brevity of my time here on earth.

You see, truth can come in many wrappings, maybe a sunset, maybe a song. But many times the written word is the most direct way for my soul to collide with truth. Simple words can remind me of an inner thirst that cannot be quenched with temporary things, and my eyes are opened once again. I need these words like oxygen; I drink them in deeply, letting them fill all of me. *New Way to be Human* offers such words; it is an alarm clock for the soul, ringing loudly, welcoming the dawn of a new day. These are words that breathe, that make me long for a heart that beats in time with the kingdom of the heavens.

My heart is twenty-seven years old now; I have much to learn and much to be thankful for. I'm grateful that the New Way to be Human is more than just a song or a book or a cause. I'm thankful for these alarm clocks that wake my soul. And I'm glad to call you my hero-friend, Charlie Peacock. For that, I appreciate that the airlines still lose our luggage.

—JON FOREMAN of Switchfoot

Prologue

The new way to be human is about the reality of God and his ways. It's about stepping into the Story of God-people-and-place with intentionality. It is the final and best opportunity to become an active participant in the community of God's people.

From the beginning of Creation, the Artist-Creator has walked with his human creation in relationship, giving them provision and meaningful word and work. His care has been consistent and sustaining. He has faithfully spoken into human history and has graciously shown people a way of life that is right and good. He has shown men and women what it means to be interested in the same things he is interested in. In return, he has asked that people trust his Word and act on it. The first living beings failed to do this, and every generation since has mistrusted God's Word. In different ways and at different times, God has dealt with our willful, chronic mistrust.

Two thousand years ago, in a last attempt at reconciliation, God sent his Son, Jesus, to earth. He entered into the fleshy side of the God-human story and let people know that the time had arrived for something entirely new. God's old way of interacting with creation was over, and a new way had begun in Jesus.

Jesus is the heir of all things, the agency of Creation, the radiance of excellence, and the exact representation of God's being. In short, he is no ordinary man. If you want to see God, you look at Jesus. If you want to hear God, you listen to Jesus. The image of God is perfect in the humanness of Jesus. In the first century, people with ears to hear and eyes to see would have known—he's what being human, living as God's direct representative, is supposed to be. People in the twenty-first century should be equally enlightened.

Jesus is the climax of God's faithful love and self-revelation. He is

Love Supreme in Word and work. There is no greater. He is the final Word of God to the human family and the embodiment of the new way to be human. Most critically, he is the means by which we enter into a renewed relationship with God. His pure and perfect cross-laden sacrifice for sin is the cure that saves us from the inevitable fruit of our mistrust and rebellion against God. Jesus saves us from missing out on the new way. He saves us into the new opportunity to be priestly human representatives in the re-creation of everything God loves.

This opportunity to be God's direct representatives in the now and everlasting is what the so-called Christian life is about. Jesus came to invite people to follow him in the making of a multinational tribe of people who love God and creation, lovers who will take God's creativity and Word seriously.

Despite the overwhelming human opinion and evidence to the contrary, Jesus did not come to start a new religion. He did not come to create a two-hour-on-Sunday parasite culture that pious people can stick on the side of their otherwise busy lives. Jesus came to subvert every aspect of life and culture with the relational Word and will of God—what he announced as *the kingdom*. The kingdom, or God's rule, is what brings a person's life into alignment with reality. To live in the kingdom way is to live a real and everlasting life, beginning the very moment you follow Jesus. This means that everything is overhauled or restructured to fit the kingdom way, the new way to be human. Knowledge, education, romance, marriage, sex, parenting, work, play, money, ambition, business, social services, caring for the earth, even being the church in the world—all of these areas and a thousand more now come under kingdom rule and authority. Following Jesus faithfully means seeing to it that all of these areas in our lives are subverted by the kingdom and rebuilt in the new way. The mission of this book is to help people reach this good goal.

You don't have anything
if you don't have the stories.

—LESLIE MARMON SILKO, *Ceremony*

Invitation

Parachute Epiphanies

Several years ago I spoke at a small Christian liberal arts college in eastern Tennessee. Afterward I joined the host professor, a half-dozen students, and my Art House compatriots for food and discussion at a nearby restaurant. A bright though anxious young man, full of story, sat across from me. He wanted to talk, to tell me at least three things. One, that he was wrestling with the form of Christianity common to his college (call it Pentecostal fundamentalism and foundationalism). Two, he was in the middle of acquiring a problem with the trustworthiness of words in general, but specifically those of the Bible and how they were interpreted on his campus. And three, he had questions about knowledge itself—how we know what we know. After rambling on about religious fundamentalism, deconstructive literary theory, and postmodern philosophy, he finally reached a climax of frustration. "Don't you see," he exclaimed. "Words have no meaning!"

To which I replied, "In that case, I haven't understood a word you've said."

"What?" he asked.

"In that case, I haven't understood a word you've said," I repeated.

Of course I'd understood him, and after a healthy pause for reflection, I let him know as much. (Note: I'm not proud of my initial retort.) This sincere student had no intention of speaking so honestly just to have me dismiss him or tell him his words were meaningless. With emotion and frustration (and words) he wanted to convey meaning—to be heard, known, and understood. He invited me into his story in all its messiness and clearly wanted me to know the questions that haunted him:

Does God really exist? If so, is God even somewhat accurately represented by the words and propositions of the group of believers I find myself tangled up with? In other words, are their ways of being, knowing, speaking, and doing congruent with God's desire for the human family? And if they are congruent, and this is who God is and what being human is, can I accept it? Or should I keep searching? And if I do speak out loud that I still haven't found what I'm looking for, does that have to mean I'm somehow unfaithful or that I don't believe?

While he wrestled with questions such as these, the young man was also trying to make sense of living in a world filled with individualized interpretations of reality where any professed certainty or confidence is the mark of a fool at best and a tyrant at worst. He'd taken a look at language through the lens of deconstructive literary theory, transposed this to philosophy, applied it to the whole of life, and now, from where he stood, God was starting to look a little unnecessary.

The young man was growing increasingly certain that all claims of certainty were only plays for power and autonomous control of people and the planet (maybe even especially so among Christians). He shouted out, "Words have no meaning!" not because they actually have none, but because they have too many, more than any one person could ever keep up with. He had begun to see that words and stories (thought units composed of words) could have as many possible meanings as there are people to construct individualized interpretations of reality. He'd come to college full of religious certainty. Now he was on the verge of giving up hope of ever finding any trustworthy, life-defining knowledge. I really did understand him. The problem of God and words is an ancient one, going all the way back to the beginning.

A few years later in 1998, when President Clinton uttered his now famous reply, "It depends on what the meaning of the word *is* is," I thought back to this young man's story and struggle. If the world really has become an infinity of individualized interpretations of reality, right down to the smallest of verbs, then perhaps the young man was prophetically distressed. Did he, wandering in the wilderness of East Tennessee, have a vision of a day when the brain twists of academia would become presidential sound bites on 24/7 cable news?

I think of him again now, wondering if he gave up the search for truth, for personal knowledge, for the Story that explains life and reality better than all others.

I wonder if he has a girlfriend, a wife, children.

What work and play does he enjoy?

When was the last time he had a party thrown for him?

And what about the words? How does he think of them today? Has he decided that they're necessary social constructs, liquid in meaning, separated into public and private sectors? Has he abandoned them altogether, preferring the certainty of silence? Or has he, like me, resolved to work with the pesky things despite how inadequate they can be from time to time?

I'm not ready to do away with words. Neither am I ready to do away with stories or the idea that trustworthy knowledge is out there and accessible. I still need words and stories. Especially when they're arranged in such a way that after speaking, writing, reading, or hearing them, I feel more human, more eager to live, not less. I desire the same for my hearers and readers—more life, not less. I imagine being a man who works with life-giving words and stories. That's the dream and the reason why I get up every morning to practice the work of imagining, creating, and telling—hoping and trusting that some of it will have life, breath, and brightness.

A brief pause for belief and confession: I confess that I hunger to be eager for life, to be fully human. I confess that I appreciate words that increase this hunger. I confess a belief in the existence of ways of being, knowing, feeling, thinking, imagining, and doing that promote a fullness of life and humanity, *and* I confess a belief in the existence of ways that do not. In short, I believe antithesis is real.

Still, I believe that words reflect their human users—they're never perfect. They are human words. The world is filled with imperfect people using imperfect language to describe imperfect human thoughts and actions. This, I believe, *is* one of life's certainties. I wonder if my friend from East Tennessee would concede to this.

I need these imperfect words in all their shapes and sizes, whether timid, bold, or humble. All manner and variety have helped me navigate the darkness and the deep. I am certain that Bob Dylan and Bono have, in words, issued warnings about storms and rough seas. I'm just as certain that Wendell Berry and Dallas Willard have, through imperfect words, helped me identify navigational errors and make course corrections. I'm certain that the theologian-apologist Francis Schaeffer once radioed me with new, lifesaving coordinates. I'm equally certain that songwriter David Wilcox and writer Brennan Manning have guided me away from the danger of shallow waters, while writer Anne Lamott helped me appreciate and celebrate the good, the strange, and the difficult I've experienced in various ports of call.

Sometimes "wordy" navigational help, like that of the people just mentioned, can be the most practical aid of all: It helps you bail water while waiting for rescue. And sometimes, in my experience, help like this *is* the means of rescue. Again and again the words and stories of poets, preachers, and pontificating Irish rock stars offer a reassuring "I hear you" to my cries for help bouncing off God's satellite. And when they do, I don't think about how shabby the words are. I think about how life-giving they are, even in their weakness.

Borrowing from a device I've heard pastor-theologian André Resner use, "I'd like ten minutes back" with my troubled college student, the East Tennessee Wilderness Prophet. Is there anyone you'd like ten minutes back with?

If I could have ten minutes back with the Prophet, I'd say this: "Close your eyes, friend, and imagine. You're high up in the air, in an aisle seat, looking past your neighbor and out the window. Down below you is a mass of cloud cover looking like fresh snow, marbled, marked with divots and craggy monuments of white. Imagine that your understanding of reality is defined by this view: what you see out the window and what's proximate to you there in the plane's cabin. The airplane and its passengers are what you might call a small, unique closed system moving inside what appears to be vast space with a visible boundary of white mass below."

Many well-meaning Christians, gathered together in various sects, present Christianity in just this way. They invite you to view reality from a very small window, and they are quite certain they're providing you with an *absolutely objective view of reality*. If you join them, you are expected to see as the sect sees. Failure to embrace their view of reality is sometimes commensurate with failure to be a follower of Jesus. And when people say you're not a follower and you are, it is very hurtful—and very troubling. For sects such as these, "anything other than absolute, unqualified, mathematically certifiable certainty betrayed a soul adrift."[1]

Let's imagine some more. Get out of your seat, reach into the compartment above, and carry the yellow package to the rest room. It's a parachute. Strap it on. Now go to the big door with the red sign, open it, and jump. When you pass through the white stuff, pull the cord.

As you pass through the clouds, down below, previously hidden from your view, is a world of wonder and wickedness, joy and pain, sex, truth, and lies. It's a place full of story upon story where words are as plentiful as stars in the sky. And there's land and promise. Land where God walked. Land belonging to him, promise belonging to him. It's a place where men and women, boys and girls, either serve themselves or serve the God of the land and the sky and all that ever was and is. This land and sea, this earth and water, is the jazz of God and humanity: order and improvisation, beauty and ashes, boundary and freedom, choice and counterchoice, mistakes and all. It is a place of storytelling and storied living.

When your feet touch the ground, look up. Do you see the plane? No? But it's there, isn't it? You know it exists; you've just come from there. Remember this: You know about the little sect's story, but they don't know about the one you just dropped into, do they? At least they don't act like it.

Now the hard work begins. At first you will feel compelled to throw out everything the little sect taught you. In fact, this is what you started to do when you encountered deconstructive literary theory and postmodern philosophy, isn't it? It feels like the answer, but it's not wise.

Over the years I've had several of these parachute epiphanies. With each one, the view widened and the clouds parted. I could see more of the Story, the one that was always there but had been obscured or hidden for various reasons.

My dream is that student-followers of Jesus will learn to tell the God-human-earth-and-sky Story with the widest, clearest view right from the beginning. I write, hoping there's a way to guide new student-followers into a rich awareness of the Story without having them feel that since they've heard and believed, they now know it all. What will it take to accomplish this? I'm not sure, but I'm on the path, watching and listening for clues, putting one foot in front of the other.

I handle each clue with care and excitement, like a child who finds a special stone along the seashore. I'm eager to show it to others, to see what the tribe thinks, feels, and says. It's slow work, but I'm growing accustomed to the pace—to what is a communal and storied way of knowing.

~

When I used to hang out with drunks and addicts, they would say, "More will be revealed." When I started hanging out with Christians, no one talked like that, or lived like that. They were largely a people of dry, almost mathematical certainty. The only time mystery entered in was when someone quoted 1 Corinthians 2:9, "No eye has seen, no ear has heard, no mind has conceived what God has prepared for those who love him."

The mystery was all eschatological, a question mark in the great by-and-by. I wish my first Christian friends had been more like the recovering drunks and addicts and had just told me, "Hey, there's a good deal of mystery in the here and now, too. More will be revealed." Maybe they weren't keeping it from me; maybe they just didn't know another way.

But you knew, didn't you, Wilderness Prophet? You were on to something back then with your questions, skepticism, fist pounding, and youthful unrest. It was T. S. Eliot who said that "doubt and uncertainty are merely a variety of belief." Did you get it sorted out? Did you come to understand that you can still be a student-follower of Jesus and not possess all truth, once-for-all universal certainty, and the answer to every question? I hope so. Especially since such things are beyond the scope of humanity, even Christian humans. Did you eventually realize that no matter how much you know, there will always be a gap in your knowledge, and therefore always mystery? Did you come to recognize the role of faith in all knowing? Did you find community where the Jesus way of life is practiced so that the way might be formed in you? And most important, do you see that you can admit gaps in knowledge and still hold that the biblical Story explains reality best? It's an unfolding Story with a sufficient starting place for knowledge, and it doesn't position itself as being exhaustive. Part of the

Story is that *only* the Creator-Storyteller holds exhaustive knowledge. This is the part that so many followers of Jesus get wrong.

I hope you've come to understand what was going on with those people who grieved and confused you so much in college. Here's what I suspect happened. Christian folk have often claimed to know too much. We've been guilty of speaking with far too much certainty. Well-meaning Christians have lived and spoken as if they've come to know what they know from someplace outside of history, outside of any cultural or social conditioning. They load you up with words, propositions, assertions, and acculturated behaviors, and then send you out as some sort of fleshy trump card to the gazillion other cards in the human deck—an agent of the gospel in the soul-saving business.

Then there comes a day when you parachute through the clouds and find out that this kind of hysterical optimism is the result of rationalism, Enlightenment dualism, and socially conditioned behavior—not necessarily what Jesus had in mind when he said to his first disciples, "Follow me." When you find out, you're relieved, but you're also angry. And with good reason, since it doesn't have to be this way. We need more parachute epiphanies on the front end, more clouds parting, no small sects in the sky on an exclusive charter flight. The growing tribe is too huge for such small thinking, for such a small epistemology.

You were on to something back then, maybe just too wounded and vulnerable to sort it out. Did you finally meet the perfect Word? Did you encounter the Word who is neither construct nor interpretation? Did you meet the Word who is the standard-bearer, the Word who overrides and governs the multiplicity of subjective words? Did you come face to face with the Word who begins the Story, sits at its center, and provides its climax? Did you meet the Word whose tribe looks through an ever-increasingly larger window—a multinational community that shares a defining, foundational loyalty to the Word made flesh? This tribe is the Community of Invitation and shows itself as such by embodying the inviting, new way to be human that the Word incarnates. This is the only tribe worthy of your image-bearing humanity. It's a fit.

When this tribe goes off course, and it does, it's always because the Word of God (the Story) has been wrongly interpreted by student-followers of the Word made flesh (Jesus), misrepresented as something it is not, or simply ignored and disregarded.

Try this on for size: The Bible is not an exhaustive record of a Tri-personal dialogue between the Father, Son, and Holy Spirit. The Bible is far from exhaustive with respect to the knowledge of God. It does not reveal with radical clarity everything there is to know about God, or all that ever was, is, or will be with respect to what is seen or unseen. Neither does it claim to, and Christians end up looking like fools when they make claims for the Bible that it doesn't make for itself.

What the Bible is, is revelation from God in the form of an accommodation to our human capacities. It takes into consideration our imperfection, our enmity with the Creator, and our failure to be what he has made us to be. It is God condescending to use human language and images from creation to bring us into a personal encounter with him. He uses human language to make his relational will as Creator clearly known, to make clear what has gone wrong between himself, humanity, and his creation, and to reveal his plan of reconciliation through the Word, the final Word to the human family: the Messiah. Jesus is the promise made good, the Word incarnate, the exact representation of God's being, revealing his character and nature.

In short, God has spelled it all out in a Story, in our world, on our behalf, for our good.

My hope is that you've come to see that it's possible to believe that the Bible (the Story) is not an exhaustive record of the knowledge of God *and* still hold to an unchanging belief that the Bible is truthful and reliable in all that it affirms. And see that it's not only possible but good to delineate that the Bible's truthfulness and reliability are dependent on its being rightly interpreted. As theologian David Clyde Jones says, "It is the God-intended meaning of Scripture as expressed in the Spirit-inspired words that is inerrant, and not some other meaning that anybody thinks the words convey."[2]

It's time for Christians to recover from the illusion of personal objectivity and the posture of unflinching certainty in every regard. These are untenable positions. *What we can say and do is hold to the Word of God as objective and absolute while confessing that our reflections on the Word are, by their very nature, relative and subjective.* This is honest orthodoxy. We can make it our goal as student-followers to interpret, reflect, and live in ways that are congruent with the intended meaning of the Bible (the Story). We can be quick to admit our failures when we don't, and we can recover from incongruent ways more quickly by not gripping our interpretations and social conditioning with an iron fist. If student-followers would live this way, old words such as *charity* could have new life and application—a leniency in judging as we all sort it out.

Instead of a my-way-or-the-highway attitude, perhaps Christians could communicate something like this: We're sure of some things, so we speak with certainty about those things. But there's a lot we're not sure of, so we're trying not to speak with certainty about those things. Please forgive us when we confuse the two. In fact, that's one of the things we're certain about: We get confused, make errors, and sin against God by claiming to know things we don't.

The best we can do is (1) make a confession, and (2) offer an invitation. One, we confess we have a starting place for looking at life. We hold to a controlling Story that makes the most sense, that explains reality best. Two, we invite you to come over and stand where we're standing at the starting place of who and what we're sure of—Jesus. We invite you to stand within our community, to stand within our story. See if what we claim to be confident of doesn't reveal to you, a human person on this planet, something you didn't know or couldn't believe before. See if we aren't modeling a new way to be human that tugs at your sense of what human destiny is. See if the window widens and the clouds begin to part. See if the Word comes to you, spinless and perfect, the best thoughts on the most important things, spoken *and* embodied. See if the Word doesn't offer to reconcile you to God, to yourself, to other people, and to the creation. See if the Word doesn't offer forgiveness and empathy for the human problem.

If life *does* look different from where we stand, and you want the reconciliation, meaning, and purpose the Word offers, then *come and see* on a day-to-day basis. Come join us in building a new worldwide community of people who take the Word seriously and are trying to live out the new way to be human that the Word teaches.

In 2000 I heard Anne Lamott speak at the Festival of Faith and Writing in Grand Rapids, Michigan. That evening I personally voted her Theologian of the Year. Sitting there in the bleachers, transported by her words, I pulled the cord on my parachute and dropped down to where she was standing, at the starting place of what she was sure of, and I saw afresh that what she claimed was certain, I, too, claimed as certain, and we were of the same tribe—a huge, ever-expanding tribe.

"Jesus," she said. "He's all I'm really sure of."

Jesus, the certain Word—a confidence that will be richly rewarded.

The Jazz of God

Ten minutes with the East Tennessee Wilderness Prophet is a beginning, not an end. Storytelling and storied living take time. I would need more time with the Wilderness Prophet for word and work, telling and showing, speaking and acting. I would need it with anyone who was genuinely interested in being a friend, in having a look at life from where I stand. Even if the standing is an audition, it gives people the necessary time to try on my location. It lets them see what things look like from a new angle—standing inside the Story as far as I understand it.

Jesus, like everyone who wears the flesh, is a man with a Story. Millions upon millions are certain of his Story. Even for skeptics and cynics, he is the return of the single defining fact. But when Jesus stepped into history, what word, what Story was he certain of? What Story did he believe he was participating in?

It doesn't matter whether I'm confused and unsure like the East Tennessee Wilderness Prophet, a novice spiritual traveler, or someone with a heart full of certainties. If I'm serious about following Jesus as his student, I should know the Story he was sure of. Following means stepping into his controlling, explanatory Story.

Luke's gospel tells the Story of Jesus and the two disciples on Emmaus Road. Luke 24:27 says, "And beginning with Moses and all the Prophets, he [Jesus] explained to them what was said in all the Scriptures concerning himself." Jesus told stories in the context of the larger Story he and his Jewish contemporaries already knew—The Book of Beginnings, the Law, the Prophets, the Wisdom Books, and Songs.

Jesus knew the Story he had stepped into. His follower Matthew knew too. Matthew started his gospel account with, "A record of the genealogy of Jesus Christ the son of David, the son of Abraham" (1:1). It's an account of the genesis of Messiah Jesus, his beginnings, his origins. Matthew 1:17 says, "Thus there were fourteen generations in all from Abraham to David, fourteen from David to the exile to Babylon, and fourteen from the exile to the Christ."

Why begin with genealogy? Matthew's message is: "Get this first. You won't fully understand what I'm about to tell you unless you have the right starting place. If you really want to understand Jesus, you have to know the Story in which he's participating (and is in fact the climax of). If you know this, you will know better how to participate, and you'll be less likely to find yourself inside the wrong story or in an insufficient one."

If Matthew's words suggest a norm for telling the Jesus Story, then *there is a serious problem with the way we invite people into the Jesus community.* Even more to the point, there's a problem with our present, basic starting place for what it means to be a student-follower. Put another way, we are storytelling humans living in a world full of stories, and there's a problem with the stories we tell one another. For example, because I tell you one story and not another, you may become one kind of follower and not another, and that could be tragic. It could mean that you might never speak and act in this world as God intended you to.

This puts a heavy burden on the place of story in life, doesn't it? But that's exactly as it should be and exactly what the Bible does. In truth, we can say that the Bible seems to bet on story—God's Story of his interaction with a people in a place. This doesn't diminish the power of God's Spirit, because the Spirit works within the story to bring enlightenment.

Writer Marva Dawn once asked her readers to "notice that the faith

the people of Israel recounted to their children was a communal one—
not so much the testimony common today of one's personal relationship
with God, but rather a witness to the way in which God has led and dealt
with the community."[1]

I agree with her. The goal is to tell a community story before you tell
a personal story. Speaking of children in the church, Dawn writes, "It is
essential that we immerse our children in the Christian faith, the belief of
a community that goes back to Abraham and Sarah, Mary and John, and
that stretches throughout the globe. We don't so much seek to develop in
them their own faith as to make them an active part of the faith that
already exists in a people."[2]

People who step into their role in the ongoing faith story of God's
people become the kind of followers Jesus desires. People who hear and
believe the Story that following Jesus is about developing your own personal faith and receiving your own personal salvation miss out on what
following Jesus actually means. Jesus calls people to follow him in the
making of a multinational tribe of Spirit-empowered people who will love
God's creativity and take his Word seriously. He's looking for people who
will exchange their agendas for God's. He's looking for kingdom representatives who through unceasing word and work will make God's rule
known everywhere and in everything.

⚊⚋⚊

In the born-again era of the 1970s and '80s, Christians would ask perfect
strangers: "Have you accepted Jesus Christ as your personal Savior?" This
question was a common starting point for evangelism, and still is in many
circles. What exactly do people mean by this question and its variations?

The book of John records that Jesus told his Jewish audience, "I tell you
the truth, whoever hears my word and believes him [the Father] who sent
me has eternal life and will not be condemned; he has crossed over from
death to life" (5:24). Here Jesus was speaking to individuals, making salva-

tion personal. Whoever hears and believes is saved from condemnation and death and is given eternal life instead. Jesus told this same group of Jews, "I have come in my Father's name, and you do not accept me" (5:43).

From these texts and others, Christians developed an efficient shorthand means of communicating the need to accept Jesus's Story about himself. In place of the word *accepted,* people often use the word *received,* as in "Have you received Jesus Christ as your personal Savior?" In 1 Corinthians 15:3, Paul wrote, "For what I received I passed on to you as of first importance: that Christ died for our sins according to the Scriptures." Paul the great evangelist received a message of first importance, and Christians rightly see Paul's message as a message others need to receive as well. The gospel of John says, "Yet to all who received him, to those who believed in his name, he gave the right to become children of God" (1:12). To receive Jesus is to welcome him. "Have you received Jesus Christ as your personal Savior?" became a shorthand way of evangelizing, of stating propositions and asking questions. If a person answered no to the question, he or she would more than likely hear something like the following:

"All people are sinners who have fallen short of the glory of God. In order to get to heaven and enjoy eternal life, your sins must be forgiven. You can only be forgiven if you confess to God that you are a sinner and receive his free gift of salvation by accepting Jesus Christ as your personal Lord and Savior. Jesus died on the cross for you and took upon himself the just punishment for your sins. He was buried and rose again on the third day. The grave could not hold him. Having conquered sin and death, he ascended to the right hand of the Father where he is now ever ready to intercede for you if you will accept him and receive him as your Lord and Savior."

When Christians talk like this, they're doing theology. That is, they're putting together organized human reflection and commentary on a portion of God's self-revelation. It follows a particular story line and has a unique emphasis. They are telling one story and not another. This Story and emphasis, when accepted as the basic foundation of Christianity, sets the tone for a unique version of the Christian life. It causes a person to become one kind of follower and not another. It becomes the standard by which a person aligns his life. At the very least, it becomes the standard for one's spiritual component or category of life.

My question is: Is this theology a truthful, comprehensive enough controlling story to define the life of someone who professes to be a student-follower of Jesus? The question isn't whether it is true, but is it the whole truth and nothing but the truth? I don't think it is. You can be assured I'm not calling into question the human need for a Savior found in Christ alone (nor am I challenging justification or substitutionary atonement). If I was starting to make you nervous, please relax. What concerns me is the kind of life Christians model for one another and the watching world when they believe that this *is* a comprehensive, meaningful theology. Here's a story that will help to illustrate why I'm challenging this theology.

I was preparing to preach on this topic, and in one of those lost moments of staring into nothing, a nursery rhyme came to me—"Jack and Jill" to be exact. I quietly whispered it to myself:

> Jack and Jill went up the hill
> To fetch a pail of water.
> Jack fell down and broke his crown
> And Jill came tumbling after.

Here are four of the simplest, most famous lines of verse in American history. What would you say "Jack and Jill" is about? I'd say that this is a story of two people traveling to get water and having an accident. But what if "Jack and Jill" is about

1. the partnership of male and female in the day-to-day needs of life?

2. the admission of human need (water), and how, in this world, meeting needs is often very difficult, dangerous work?

3. the topography of life where there are hills and valleys, and sometimes you climb a hill just to fall back down again?

4. the fact that human actions with the best of intentions for the purest of needs can still end in tragedy?

5. the ineptitude of men, and how they drag women down with them? (Just kidding, I think.)

What if "Jack and Jill" is about all of this (and more), *and* it is about two people traveling to get water and having an accident?

What we think the story is about depends a good deal on where we stand as we read it or observe it. Our ways of knowing, being, and doing are not neutral. Neither is the family, the community, or the nation we stand within.

What if Christianity is about humans as sinners in need of a Savior, but like "Jack and Jill," it is about so much more? What if the "so much more" is just as important as the fact that we are sinful humans in need of a Savior? What if it's the "so much more" that provides the controlling Story for unceasing life beginning right now? To miss something as important as the controlling Story would be to miss the script, the operating instructions, the way to be human.

When the "personal Savior" story gets mixed together with individualism and consumerism, a nasty liaison is born. This combination has shaped the lives of men and women into something quite different than what Jesus had in mind when he called the disciples to follow him. This unfortunate triad has led many to a highly subjective spirituality, one scarcely able to attract or sustain interest in people who interact with it.

In case you are a reader who is still nervous or doesn't yet understand where I'm going with all of this, don't be confused. If anybody needed a Savior when I met Jesus, I did (and still do, thank you). I don't disagree with the reality of personal sin and the need for forgiveness and personal salvation. And I believe that salvation is possible only by grace through faith in Christ alone. I also see the connection between this language and the ideas found in Scripture regarding the heart as the focus of belief (Romans 10:9), the notion of receiving Jesus (John 1:12), and what one must do to be saved (Acts 16:31).

Still, I often wonder, *Why didn't somebody tell me the whole Story and invite me to participate in it?* Our usual contemporary method of telling the Jesus Story has focused far more on saving people *from* hell than saving them *to* unceasing life with God. Our language and approach reflect the Reformation and post-Reformation traditions (Puritanism, Pietism, evangelicalism) as well as nineteenth-century revival technique. The Reformation and its aftershocks did (properly, I think) make faith more personal and less corporate in so far as they put an end to the abuses common to the church at the time. The Reformers rejected all assertions that the church held any power to save, and they affirmed that there is no intermediary between God and humans except Messiah Jesus. The Reformers wisely understood that this is the *personal* aspect worth fighting for.

Over time and under various influences, Christians exchanged the totality of the invitation Jesus came to give for a smaller, more mechanical and efficient story. As a result, more often than not, an invitation to follow Jesus fails to describe the scope of redemption and renewal that Jesus set in motion and made final.

Choosing one story over another, one approach over another, has not been neutral. Privatization and individualism have robbed the community of the storied connection to God's ongoing outworking of redemptive history through Jesus. Not only have the Wilderness Prophet–types been affected and confused but so have the average pew dwellers and those who watch and listen while the community of followers speak and act. The stories we tell one another have power. Again, the story you hear when you first start following Jesus steers you toward becoming one kind of follower and not another. Knowing this, it is essential to begin with the most comprehensive Story possible.

To go no further than the God of the soul (where privatized views of Christianity usually peak) is to miss out on the sufficiently huge view of God, people, and place. You cannot put together the way to be human without knowing the Story from beginning to end. Without it, the ordering and power that lead to being human as God designed will be absent. There will be a loss of integrity. God's relational Word is what guides creational action.

~

Reading the Bible with the starting place of personal salvation alone is like reading it through the wrong end of a telescope. Read through the wrong end, it's a story about efficiency, about reducing something huge and extraordinary to something small and manageable—*get 'em saved and into heaven.* I liken it to the difference between multiple choice and essay testing. With multiple choice, you often choose the right answers because you've memorized them. Yet it's entirely possible that you can't construct the parts into a whole. You can't make sense of them so that they make sense of your subject. In an essay you either know what you're talking about or you don't. And when you don't, it's painfully obvious to anyone and everyone, including yourself.

Thankfully, sometimes the passion for following Jesus is so strong that a person circuitously finds his or her way to the larger Story—what I call "backing into it." Once arrived, he or she sees that the larger Story *is* the ordering, controlling system and that redemption (or salvation) is one of four main themes in the larger controlling Story of God, people, and planet.

When we miss this and try to convince people that the *getting saved* story is all there is, no one is fooled, especially not the bright Wilderness

Prophet–types. Our view shows itself as small, and our understanding is revealed as insufficient by the stories we tell with our lives.

In chapter 1, I confessed belief in a spiritual foundation available to all people—the best above all others—that is found in Jesus's ways of knowing, being, and doing. It is found in his Story, one I maintain is true (as in having the weight of scientific fact). Nevertheless, I've also come to realize that even if this spiritual foundation is good and admirable (made up of the best and most important stories), the story my life tells will never be better than my day-to-day embodiment of this invisible spiritual foundation. So-called *truths* without embodiment are like misty vapors drifting in the wind and then disappearing. Truths played out in hearts and hands stay. They make themselves at home. They live for the tribe, for the community. Truths that don't show and tell a way of being human that involves more love of God and neighbor, greater mercy, generosity and self-sacrifice, as well as faithful, careful stewardship of people and planet, are in my opinion not truths worth bothering with. Regarding truth, we might want to use fewer words—that is, underpromise in the language department and overdeliver in the living. The book of James helps us here:

> Do not merely listen to the word, and so deceive yourselves. Do
> what it says. Anyone who listens to the word but does not do what
> it says is like a man who looks at his face in a mirror and, after
> looking at himself, goes away and immediately forgets what he
> looks like. But the man who looks intently into the perfect law that
> gives freedom, and continues to do this, not forgetting what he has
> heard, but doing it—he will be blessed in what he does. (1:22-25)

Most of us aren't ready to write the National Merit Scholarship–equivalent essay of the Story. We can't sit down with a friend and tell the Story of God-people-and-place in a truthful, compelling way. Instead, we're more likely to be multiple-choice-type followers, unsure as to how the pieces of the Story explain or control anything other than a general pointing toward Jesus, personal salvation, and quiet times. We should not be fooled. Every student-follower of Jesus is made to be a storyteller and to have his or her way of being human informed by God's controlling narrative.

There are always stories informing and controlling human lives. Are they the right ones, the best? We can't be naive about what narratives run through our lives and shape our choices. God offers a controlling, explanatory Story to his people in his Word. If we ignore it, we will not go without a controlling story or, for that matter, many controlling stories. Some set of stories will shape our lives. We cannot escape this fact. We can live intentionally, though, and step into the God-human-earth-and-sky Story that makes more sense of life than any other.

The narrative of God acting in human history is compelling, not boring. Yet somehow many of us who profess to follow Jesus have dreamed up the most fantastic ways to rob the Story of its power to attract and invite. Do you ever wonder…

- why people who call themselves Christians are so easily caricatured?
- why Christianity is so often seen as an unattractive religion when Jesus, the person on whom it is founded, is considered to be one of the most enigmatic, compelling, and attractive figures in world history (even by critics of Christianity and/or politically conservative Christians)?
- why people who call themselves Christians have taken their place among the clichéd, bored, cynical masses as if they hold no sure means to escape or transcend such a fate?
- why the talk of professing Christians about "their faith" sounds like a mantra they've grown bored with rather than the story of something profound, mysterious, beautiful, and life-changing?

- why professing Christians can't seem to discuss "their faith" with anything near the expertise, enthusiasm, and imagination they have for hobbies, sports, celebrities, films, or music?

Marva Dawn voiced my own frustrations when she said, "One main reason why people outside of Christian spirituality aren't attracted to it is because we [Christians] don't demonstrate a way of life different enough to warrant belief. Everyone in our culture has too much to do, so why should anyone bother with becoming a student of Jesus, or going to church on Sunday mornings, if Christians do not demonstrate that following Jesus is a better way to live?"[3]

Good question. How is it that student-followers of Jesus end up with lives that don't demonstrate that following Jesus is a better way to live? How is it that we tell this kind of unattractive story, send this kind of distorted signal out across neighborhoods, cities, oceans, and international boundaries?

It happens when we rebel against and reject the Art and Story of God—when we become anti-Artist. To have the spirit of the anti-Artist is to resemble amateur painters who rush from the presence of a Michelangelo saying, "Let's get out of here, anybody can do that." Wrong. There is a God-artistry and a God-story worthy of respect, even reverence, for it is life-defining Art and Story. So much of our failure to demonstrate that following Jesus is a better way to live can be attributed to the error of trying to live outside of God's Rule, Art, and Story.

Granted, our immune systems are stressed and taxed by the pollutants of the world's ways of being, knowing, thinking, and doing. The sicker we become, the harder it is to fight off the sickness. Finally, we give up. Hearts grow cold. Boredom, indifference, and apathy set in, and even the old standby—the mask of the shiny, happy Christian—doesn't work anymore. It's replaced by the new mask of the twenty-first century—the burned-out, flat-lined, blank-faced whatever. It's different, but hardly a substitute for the brightness of God in human form. No generation of followers of Jesus should stand for this. It would be better to die attempting faithfulness than to give up, or never try at all.

In every time and in every era, it is appropriate to ask the questions, What does it mean to be a student-follower of Jesus? What does it mean to act on the calling to be, in our time, what Jesus was in his—the Israel of God? How thoroughly and convincingly do any of us speak about matters of ultimate concern? Are we able to identify what it is that gives meaning and direction to life? And once these ways are located and identified, are we able to test whether they are biblical, that is, congruent with God's ways of knowing, being, thinking, and doing?

Are we able to talk with the East Tennessee Wilderness–type people without merely confirming their worst suspicions about God's people? Do we receive any help from other Christians in learning how to do this? Does it even matter to anyone around us? I hope so. Each of us ought to ask ourselves with regularity, What is the Story that defines being human and controls the course of life? And how is this Story affecting every area of life, from sexuality to work, from friendship to what happens once this life is through?

No generation can rule out the possibility that some of what we believe to be good and biblical are the very ideas and formulas keeping us from being the light of the world and the salt of the earth. It's strange, but it happens. Sincere people can be both victims and perpetrators of various distortions having to do with God, the world, the kingdom, and what it means to be human.

Every human needs personal/relational knowledge of God not as a mental abstraction or a composite of various religions, but as a person with a personal interest. This is true spirituality. The Story of God, particularly that of Jesus, is the Story of God among us, as one of us, taking life personally. You can be sure that the Creator-Artist takes his art seriously, and that he always cares for what he loves.

My encouragement to folks like the East Tennessee Wilderness Prophet is to step into the Story. From there, walk with others who are taking it seriously. Then see if this word-and-work life doesn't make sense of the world in the best and most believable way. See if it doesn't give an account of the problem and the glory of humanity in a way that satisfies. And to those who call themselves Christians, it's always good to revisit the Story, cultivate memory, and keep it alive in every generation.

The best way to know God or people personally (to learn their ways of being and doing) is to learn of them through their own stories or self-disclosure—that is, what they've clearly revealed about themselves. Student-followers of Jesus believe that God's self-disclosure is the Bible and the creation. In order for anyone, follower or not, to truly investigate God's Story and the new way to be human that Jesus teaches, we have to go to the Bible and look around us at what we see. We have to stand in the Story—the whole Story. To remain open to the Story the Bible communicates as well as the claims it makes, we have to personally interact with them. That's only fair.

The goal of a student-follower of Jesus is to live as a knowledgeable, active participant in the kingdom agenda of God. This personal knowledge is available and comes with power from God himself. Long ago he gave his people a community knowledge. This knowledge is carried across time in every generation by a people of long memory. It's Art and Story. It's the jazz of God that Jesus stepped into—it's people and place.

<hr />

If I could have time back with the East Tennessee Wilderness Prophet, I'd tell lots of jazzy stories, but one in particular. He may have heard it before, perhaps many times. But like the rest of us, he might want to be reminded of how it unfolds, how its people and place are our story, too.

These are the basics I would start with—basics the East Tennessee Wilderness Prophet may need to think about in a new way in order to understand the Story. The Story of God-people-and-place as collected together in the Bible. The Bible is actually sixty-six short books, thirty-nine in the Old Testament and twenty-seven in the New. As comprehensive as this is, the Bible is not exhaustive. What book could be? Still, it's sufficient to communicate the way of God to people and remind those who've lost memory of it.

The Story that Jesus and his Jewish contemporaries stepped into is documented in The Law, the Prophets, and the Writings (what is known as the Old Testament today). This was their explanatory, controlling Story. The narrative contemporary to Jesus and his first disciples is documented in the New Testament books of the Bible. Together, the Old and the New Testaments form the book that reminds men and women of the ongoing Story they have stepped into since birth.

Some people step in and live intentionally, pointing their compass toward the way things are supposed to be. Others step in but fail to understand the Story in which they are participating. Competing stories distract them and work to distort the little they do know and understand. Still others deny the presence of an explanatory Story altogether, or they find another explanatory story more attractive to them.

Like any story, the Bible has a beginning and an end. In the beginning God the Creator-Artist created the heavens and the earth (Genesis 1:1). By the end of the Story, he's making everything new again (Revelation 21:1-5). In the space between, it's a long, twisting, messy trek filled with small stories, sermons, genealogies, prayers, letters, songs, poems, and proverbs of every conceivable style, incorporating every literary device from hyperbole to alliteration and acrostic to stream of consciousness. The subject matter is the whole of life, hellish and heavenly. The rhythms of God, people, and planet cross and crisscross with a noisy racket. The creative beauty of God's handiwork is mixed together in the same history with a fat king named Eglon who was murdered by a left-handed man named Ehud. And that's just the tip of it. This is the Story Jesus began, stepped into, and is now making new.

What is this huge biblical narrative in short form?

First, it's important to mention that the Story presupposes a Creator who is good, perfect, and trustworthy. The Story makes no defense for the existence of the Creator. From there I'd say it's a story about God, people, and place. Four major historical categories hold the narrative together:

Creation   *Fall*   *Redemption*   *New Creation*

Using these categories, Creation tells us what is right and good about people and heaven and earth. The Fall tells us what is wrong about them. The history of Redemption tells us what the Creator is doing to restore rightness and goodness. The New Creation is the perfect completion of the Story.

Knowing this helps us take a basic first step to remedy the problem of what kind of stories we tell one another. We can begin by returning to the creational context and then to the historical Jewish context in which Jesus told his stories and lived his storied life. That's why people study the whole Story the Bible clearly communicates. It's why they take the Bible seriously for what it is first: the Story of God-people-and-place. It's not myth or fiction but rather the Story of what was, is, and will be.

It's this narrative—from the first Creation to the New Creation—that we turn to next. Step in. It's your story, too.

The Story We
Step Into

God, People, and Place

The history of the followers of Jesus is littered with sincere but mistaken ideas about what it means to be human. The way of Jesus and the humanness he models (and offers) begins with the Story he stepped into and its way of being human—its anthropology. The first two chapters of the book of Genesis give people the help they need to understand the Creator's first choices about the way to be human.

The book of Genesis (the Book of Beginnings) begins with a Creator-God who creates everything and calls it very good. All of God's creativity has the rightness he intended for it. He embedded everything with an integrity and bias toward his agenda, for the way reality is to be shaped. In the Creation narrative God said, "Let us make man in our image, in our likeness, and let them rule over the fish of the sea and the birds of the air, over the livestock, over all the earth, and over all the creatures that move along the ground" (Genesis 1:26).

God created living beings in his image, male and female. Borrowing from Anthony Hoekema: *Man and woman are inescapably related to God.* There's a family resemblance. Not to be confused with the Creator, man and woman are creatures—earthy, sexy (if it's possible to redeem this word), and yet somehow, mysteriously family—and they have been since the very beginning.

And so it was that before there was any need for a new way to be human, Genesis revealed the way to be human.

The beginning Story of God and his people describes a norm. It's the pattern of God, land, and people—the pattern of God's people in his place, living entirely for him and by him. It is God with people and for people—the Emmanuel of Christmas right from the beginning. This norm can be divided into two parts. First, *the Creational Norm*—man and woman walk with God on earth in the garden (his place). The Creator shares his creation (his creative Word) with man and woman. Second, *the Relational Norm*—man and woman walk with God in intimate friendship (God and people). The Creator shares matters of mutual interest and importance with man and woman—his will and way (his spoken, relational Word).

In the beginning, man and woman were in right relationship with God, living with him, under his good rule, and in his good place. Man and woman functioned in harmony with holiness, goodness, and rightness. Through God's creative Word, a fruitful land was provided—a place of beauty and provision. Through God's relational Word, the way of life was provided. Man and woman were created to live under God's rule and agenda, his way of ordering life (see Genesis 2:16-17). He conferred well-being and prosperity on them (see Genesis 1:28). He gave man and woman his benediction and blessing. Death was mentioned not as a norm, but as a consequence of disobedience, of choosing contrary to God's way of ordering life. Anything contrary to God's ways would be antilife and prodeath. The Story supports the reality of antithesis.

In the beginning God created man and woman to rule over creation, to govern, to be his people in his place (see Genesis 1:26,28). Man and woman were to speak and act as direct representatives of God, as if speaking and acting for God himself. The Creator gave man and woman a cultural mandate to develop each other and the whole of earth, to rule over nature as servant-representatives. He created man and woman with reason and intelligence and called them to use these abilities (see Genesis

2:19-20). Man and woman used these abilities to work with God in bringing further order to life. With their whole being, man and woman served and governed God's good creativity.

In the beginning there was unbroken relationship in human enterprise, male-female partnership, marriage, and sex. Relationship, work, and governing were as they should be—linked exclusively to God's rightness and goodness. Man and woman were sexually differentiated and unique, yet equal and complementary to one another (see Genesis 2:18). Man and woman were created to live in relationship with others, in pairs and tribes as an earthly picture of the heavenly fellowship God has within his Tri-person.

From the beginning people were made for community. Personal fulfillment was never the goal. Every word, every gift, every movement was meant for the good of people and place and for the pronouncement of the Creator's excellence. Man and woman in their earthiness were created for complete exposure in thought, imagination, deed, and flesh. Since no threat or accusation yet existed, hiding and denial were still unknown. God and his people were in a place of God's making. God talked to creation. God talked to people. People talked to God. Prayer was conversation. Like breathing, there was not an ounce of trying.

In the beginning there was unbroken relationship to earth and sky as a hospitable place of beauty and a resource to be cultivated and multiplied. The creation yielded to the needs and creativity of humankind. Man and woman were created to live in a world of pleasure and goodness where God established a pattern of creativity that was aesthetically pleasing and useful (see Genesis 2:9). God made art that people could live with. God created man and woman to do the same. To that end, they were called to identify, discover, and explore all the resources and possibilities of the Creator's genius. They were created to be the caretakers of creativity, to have a total involvement with the good creation, to be the Creator's direct representatives on earth caring for earth and sky and all that is in them. They were called to take personally what the Creator takes personally and to maintain his kind of rightness in the creation, for the good of creation. Man and woman were made to be workers after the pattern of the Creator, with the rhythm of work and rest established by him (see Genesis 2:2,15).

Care was everywhere in the beginning. Every need was met, either by God directly, his earth and sky, or through his representatives, man and woman. Unity in diversity with freedom of choice was the norm. Man and woman were *able not to sin,* able to stay in the good, God-directed story.

~~~~

The Creation narrative in Genesis tells us that man and woman were created to bear God's image (see Genesis 1:26-27). A basic understanding of the image starts with God the Creator. He is a worker who imagines and creates. He called man and woman into existence by his imaginative and creative Word (see Genesis 1:26; 2:7a). He filled them with his life-breath (see Genesis 2:7b).

The Word is the counsel of God spreading out from God to that which he loves. The Word is Personality in control of matter. God's Word and his will are synonymous. When he creates he makes his will known. When he speaks he makes his will known. He speaks to create, and what he creates speaks. The same holds true for man and woman on a creaturely level. This is the privilege and responsibility of bearing God's image. His revelation of himself in creation is general revelation. His revelation in the Story (the Bible) is special revelation.

God's Word has creational power. He speaks with creative intentionality. He is a discerning choice maker, able to judge the quality of his choices. He chooses beautifully and perfectly as a reflection of his being. All his ways are right and good.

God's Word has relational power. He speaks and acts. He promises and fulfills his promises. He is communicative and self-giving, caring for his creation and giving it all it needs to thrive.

God is an aesthetically oriented Creator of a vast complexity of creative work, yet he is able to focus on the smallest and simplest details of caring. He makes his creations multifunctioning, such as trees that are pleasing to the eye and good for food.

Because man and woman were created to bear God's image, the way to be human involved this kind of being and doing on a creaturely level. In short, what was true of the Creator was to be true of his created representatives. This was the controlling Story set in motion by the Creator-God when he created the good and necessary conditions for life.

In Genesis we can also see that the *personal* in all of the *Christian* language about personal relationship starts with God himself as the initiator of relationship. He is the one who makes everything personal, and so takes everything personally. There is nothing impersonal about the Story in Genesis 1 and 2, or the Story in its entirety.

God created the structure for life and gave it direction with his good will, his agenda, his ways of being and doing. The will of God is good, and good is the will of God. They are one and the same. Even his one prohibition, "You must not eat" (Genesis 2:17), is not an impersonal law, but personal will in the form of a commandment.

—&#127;—

In Genesis 1 and 2 we see that God initiates relationship first by speaking. He speaks creation into being, and then sustains it by his relational word. He said he would do something, and he did. This is the first word, first promise, first covenant.

By *covenant* I mean a mutually binding relationship. Creation calls the covenant into existence, and covenant becomes the context for God, his people, and his place. Knowledge of God doesn't come from speculation but from listening to him and watching him act in history as Creator. We can hear him and see him through the amplifier and lens of his Story. Our understanding of his identity and our own is formed out of the Story.

God clearly had something good in mind when he created humans. He connected them to himself in every possible way. He even animated them with his own breath. He pointed humans in the direction of the way to be human—the way to be his people, in his place, in conversation and relationship with him. God spoke into being the way things are supposed to be in order for Creation to declare his glory, his excellence. This is the controlling, explanatory Story that Jesus knew and stepped into when the Word was made flesh. This is the history that informed and shaped his very real first-century Jewish life. Anyone who claims to follow him must be informed and shaped by it as well.

The Reality of the Fall

If Creation is the explanation for what's right with man and woman, the Fall clarifies what's wrong. The Creator included one prohibition in his personal conversation with the first living beings, saying, "You must not eat from the tree of the knowledge of good and evil, for when you eat of it you will surely die" (Genesis 2:17). Along with his loving care, God gave man and woman one mystery. He purposely created a gap in their knowledge. It was up to man and woman to trust the Creator with the unknown and to let mystery be.

In order to better understand the Fall, we need to look at a supreme attribute of God: his holiness. God's holiness is what sets him apart from us. He is morally perfect and excellent in every way. In every circumstance God does what is right. He keeps his word. He does not lie. He *is* purity and absolute moral perfection.

At the beginning of Genesis 3, the reader/hearer is introduced to a speaking creature called the serpent, one who was "more crafty than any of the wild animals the LORD God had made. He said to the woman, 'Did God really say, "You must not eat from any tree in the garden"?'" (verse 1).

This challenge was the first volley of what would become an unprecedented battle between humans and Satan. Jesus would say of Satan: "He was a murderer from the beginning, not holding to the truth, for there is no truth in him. When he lies, he speaks his native language, for he is a liar and the father of lies" (John 8:44). The crafty serpent (inhabited by Satan) was testing the woman's knowledge of the Story. He was asking,

"Do you actually know what God said?" You see what I mean about *God* and *words* being an old, old problem?

Satan's technique is to question, accuse, and distort God's clear signal. His method is to nuance a story, dismantle it, or twist it into something altogether different. This is why British author Steve Turner refers to Satan as the King of Twists. Satan twists words and stories in the hope of twisting hearts and minds. His glory is his shame, and he wants to lead others to a similar glory.

The woman told the serpent, "We may eat fruit from the trees in the garden, but God did say, 'You must not eat fruit from the tree that is in the middle of the garden, and you must not touch it, or you will die'" (Genesis 3:2-3).

The woman answered, but in answering she failed to handle the Word of God with care. She added to God's Word ("don't touch"), making it stricter than it originally was, and she omitted the fact that there were two trees in the middle of the garden. The Creator had prohibited eating from only one, the tree of the knowledge of good and evil.

Next the serpent lied, "You will not surely die.... For God knows that when you eat of it your eyes will be opened, and you will be like God, knowing good and evil" (Genesis 3:4-5). To have your eyes opened is to become wise—to see things as they really are. This is what the serpent was telling the woman would happen. But wisdom wasn't what the deceiving serpent had in mind.

The serpent revealed his agenda—to be like God and entice others to want the same. The sad thing is, man and woman were already like God! The woman's answer should have been, "We are already like God in that we alone bear his image, his likeness for his glory. As for the knowledge of good and evil, that is for God alone to know. He has not made this mystery our business, and to make it our concern is to disobey the only prohibition he's given us."

Genesis 3:6 says, "When the woman saw that the fruit of the tree was good for food and pleasing to the eye, and also desirable for gaining wisdom, she took some and ate it. She also gave some to her husband, who was with her, and he ate it."

The woman, as a created choice maker, lost track of the controlling Story line. Instead of her motive being love in relationship with God, her mate, and the earth and sky, and instead of her purpose on earth being God's glory (his good will and excellence), her motive and purpose morphed to self alone. Quickly the big world God had given her became very small and personal. Reflecting on the tree's good food and pleasing appearance, did she wonder, *How can something so good (like all the other trees in the garden) lead to death?*

It's possible that in that moment of testing, she previewed a concept of God that many have today: *God is so good he would never allow death to be the consequence of disobedience. He values life too much.* And that's exactly it. But how we interpret value depends on how we define life. Is it existence by our own standards, our own word? Or is it a quality that can only be known in right relationship with the Creator and his Word?

Perhaps the tree was like all the others, but what the woman missed was its almost sacramental function. The tree of the knowledge of good and evil was a sign and symbol of God's spoken, relational Word and will. His will was right up front with respect to the tree, but the woman overlooked the Creator, ignored his Word, and saw the creation alone. She esteemed creation more than the Creator.

You may empathize with the woman, and in the quiet of your mind voice the implicit question, *What was the knowledge of good and evil?* If this comes to you, then you know the same curiosity that motivated Eve toward disobedience: intolerance of mystery.

Maybe this is what Paul was referring to in Romans 16:19 when he said, "I want you to be wise about what is good, and innocent about what is evil" or in 1 Corinthians 14:20: "Brothers, stop thinking like children. In regard to evil be infants, but in your thinking be adults."

The prohibition was meant to ensure that God's people *would be wise* about what is good, and innocent about what is evil. The woman confused the human-centered activity of gaining factual information with the gaining of wisdom. Wisdom is God-centered and comes by God's giving his good will to his people. Wisdom is *his mind* about what is actually pertinent to being human and living within the good will. The Creator has the authority to limit knowledge, to give us what is sufficient if not exhaustive. He remains the caretaker of mystery for his own purposes. Which is why the wise writer said in Psalm 131: "My heart is not proud, O LORD, my eyes are not haughty; I do not concern myself with great matters or things too wonderful for me" (verse 1).

What we have here is the Story's first epistemological problem, a problem of knowledge, that is, how humans know what they know. The Story's answer to how humans know what they know is the image of God within, and their storied relationship with God himself. They are knowers after the pattern of God, and all their knowing is regulated by God's creative and controlling Story—his will, his rightness, and his goodness. The relationship with God always defines the use of human intelligence. Knowing comes from the life he gives, from the relationship he shares (the Way, the Truth, and the Life was on the scene from the very beginning). The accumulation of so-called knowledge or wisdom that doesn't serve the God-human relationship and the mission of humans on earth is of no true value. The Prophets had something to say to this. Isaiah said: "Your wisdom and knowledge mislead you when you say to yourself, 'I am, and there is none besides me'" (47:10). Jeremiah said: "The wise will be put to shame; they will be dismayed and trapped. Since they have rejected the word of the LORD, what kind of wisdom do they have?" (8:9).

There is no wisdom in replacing God's Word with another word, or with anything for that matter. It is the worst of exchanges. As the book of Romans says: "They exchanged the truth of God for a lie, and worshiped and served created things rather than the Creator" (1:25).

Genesis goes on to describe how the woman also "gave some [fruit] to her husband, who was with her, and he ate it" (3:6). The woman was second in creation but first in sin. Once the perfect finish to God's Creation and the helpful answer to what was not complete with man, the woman helped the man begin his own disobedience. Instead of helping man with his aloneness, she aided him in becoming more alone. He became alienated from the woman, God, and all of creation. It is said that only in woman is the Creation complete, and only in man is the Fall complete. So it was. What began with him ended with him. Man was first in creation and second in sin, but he was first in responsibility. He heard the story first.

After eating the fruit, Genesis 3:7 says, "Then the eyes of both of them were opened, and they realized they were naked; so they sewed fig leaves together and made coverings for themselves."

Having disconnected themselves from the life of God's Word, they tore fig leaves from the life of a tree and set in motion premature decomposition. The leaves withered and died, turned stiff, and became brittle. Man and woman looked to creation as a cure for their shame. They used the leaves as a way of covering up their sexual, physical differences, a way of hiding from each other in their complete exposure. But creation then and now is no cure for shame. Relationship is no cure for shame, and neither is the caretaking/dominion role. The first man and woman found this out, and every generation since then has tested it, hoping to be the one that finds the cure in someone or something other than God.

Next, "the man and his wife heard the sound of the LORD God as he was walking in the garden in the cool of the day, and they hid from the LORD God among the trees of the garden" (Genesis 3:8).

Hiding from the Creator? Yes, and sadly, trees that were once good for food and pleasing to the eye were used to hide from God. First the leaves, now the trees. Sin always distorts the good use of creation. A pattern was set in motion.

God addressed his first question to the man: "Where are you?" (verse 9). The question showed that God held man responsible. The man answered, "I heard you in the garden, and I was afraid because I was naked; so I hid" (verse 10).

Fear arrived on the scene as a new emotion for people. Man, intimately known by his Creator, was now afraid of being known, of being revealed as he really was, the one who disobeyed, the one who was guilty, the one who knew shame. It's said that fear produces fight or flight. This first move of hiding was flight. Next came the fight. The Creator asked the man, "Who told you that you were naked? Have you eaten from the tree that I commanded you not to eat from?" (verse 11).

To hear God ask "Who told you?" was to also hear the unspoken message, *I didn't tell you—your knowledge of this did not come from me.*

The man said, "The woman you put here with me—she gave me some fruit from the tree, and I ate it" (verse 12).

The woman wasn't just put there, she was created out of him and for him as the glorious climax to human Creation, and the man was intimately involved in body and mind. Alienation crept into the garden. Notice how the man said "with me" instead of "*for* me." He had already diminished her role. The man was distancing himself from reality, the true Story. Not only did he misplace God's Word, he forgot his own. How long had it been since he'd exclaimed: "*This is* now bone of my bones, flesh of my flesh. *This is why* a man will (in the future) leave his father and mother, because woman alone is the answer to the help I need!"

It was all gone—amnesia had set in.

"She gave me some fruit...and I ate it." He was there! Was he saying that the only reason he ate it was because she had handed it to him?

"Then the LORD God said to the woman, 'What is this you have done?'" (verse 13).

It's as if God were saying, *"I've heard his testimony, now let me hear it from you."*

So the woman spoke: "The serpent deceived me, and I ate" (verse 13).

Good. Hers was a far better answer than his. Looking ahead to future words, others who walk with God will agree:

For sin, seizing the opportunity afforded by the commandment, deceived me, and through the commandment put me to death. (Romans 7:11)

But I am afraid that just as Eve was deceived by the serpent's cunning, your minds may somehow be led astray from your sincere and pure devotion to Christ. (2 Corinthians 11:3)

Since both the man and woman ended their accounts with "I ate," there was no doubt that they both knew their culpability. Since "don't eat" summed up the prohibition, "I ate" stood as a confession.

Just as rightness and goodness affect the whole person, so does sin. Instead of being inescapably related to God in right relationship, the man and woman became inescapably disconnected from the Creator and seemingly inescapably connected to sin.

~⁓~

Sin by definition is rebellion against God's Word—his Story of the way things ought to be. Cornelius Plantinga Jr. defines *sin* as "a culpable disturbance of shalom."[1] Sin is a change of direction away from the peace and rightness of God's ways toward an assumption that humankind can and should define life on its own. The thoughts and actions we see in the man and woman at the Fall became a part of the couple. The sinful way of knowing, being, and doing became their nature and the nature of every person to come into the world since—with the exception of Jesus. Sin had attacked human, creational integrity and distorted the way to be human. The man and woman were exposed and ashamed. Sin had alienated them from their Creator. They were slaves to sin. Guilt was real, and death and punishment awaited man and woman.

Following the Story line, the Creator described the consequences of the serpent's behavior:

So the LORD God said to the serpent, "Because you have done this,

"Cursed are you above all the livestock
    and all the wild animals!
You will crawl on your belly
    and you will eat dust
    all the days of your life.
And I will put enmity
    between you and the woman,
    and between your offspring and hers;
he will crush your head,
    and you will strike his heel." (Genesis 3:14-15)

This was both a curse and a foretelling word from God. Some un-mentioned offspring of the woman would one day crush the Father of Lies, the King of Twists. The Story had only just begun.

Because God is holy, he cannot tolerate sin in any form. Because he is holy, he judges justly. He pronounced his judgments and drove the couple out of his place (the perfect setting of Eden) to a cursed and much less hospitable place east of Eden. As history proves, it is a grievous mis-take to have anything other than a sober view of the holiness of God.

Because of the first couple's disobedience and rebellion against God, the human family and all of creation are now corrupt in every way. No part of a human being or creation is untouched by sin and evil. People experience a total corruption of their humanity. When I say total, I mean pervasive. I'm describing the scope of the effects of sin in that no part of humanity remains untouched. It's often explained this way: No part of humanity is as bad as it could be, yet no part is as good as it should be.

Our physical well-being is under attack. We are subject to disease, decay, and death. We use our imagination and intellect to twist words and situations, rationalizing and making absurd excuses for our sin and failure. We are guilty before God and alienated from him—friendship and fellowship are broken. Every human relationship and enterprise is affected by sin, from sex and family to business and international relations. Because of sin, the earth itself is under God's curse. Though called to care for it, we remain frustrated by our environment. It is never totally subdued. Everything we create is subject to decay.

While waiting for rescue we continue to work, imagine, and create. Though we are choice makers, we're often incapable of judging the quality of our choices except by a measure of self-interest. Communication and relationship are the victims of self-interest as well. Man and woman, dependent on God and responsible to him, have become independent and irresponsible. The worship due the Creator is given to the creation instead, to idols of self, relationship, achievement, and money. Mutual fulfillment, fellowship, and community have given way to personal fulfillment, isolation, and an army of one. Domination for the purpose of glorifying oneself has replaced the dominion-calling to serve and care for God's creativity.

Things are not the way they are meant to be—not at all. This is a fact, a science-type fact. The way to be human given by God to man and woman for pleasure and purpose is twisted up by sin. Sin is not religion or a value or a preference in belief. It is—like air and water—very, very real.

Life East of Eden

The Story continues after the first couple's disobedience, but sin is now the new degraded direction of humankind—that is, a movement away from the love of God, the Word of God, the will of God, the original controlling Story. Man and woman are no longer holy or right. The family intimacy they once knew with God and each other is broken.

Exiled from the Garden of Eden, the human family grew—children came into the world, and the pattern of sin and disintegration that began with the Fall continued. Human death finally came in the form of murder when a son, Cain, killed his brother, Abel.

The East of Eden culture has two categories (or lines) of humanity, both fallen: (1) those who do not listen and obey God's relational Word, those who have no love for God or brother (neighbor), those who create gods of their own imagination or, like Cain, try to come to the one true God in their own way; and (2) those who, like Abel, listen and obey God's relational Word, who come to him as he prescribes.

After the death of Abel, Eve gave birth to another son, Seth, and he continued in the line of Abel. Both the line of Cain and the line of Seth were active on the earth. Humanity became more and more evil, with sin like a compass setting the course for all of life. Some exceptions existed, such as Enoch (in the line of Seth) who "walked with God." Eventually only one man was left who walked with God: Noah (also in the line of Abel and Seth). God was about to judge sin, but he gave grace to one man, and through this one man a family was saved.

The LORD saw how great man's wickedness on the earth had
become, and that every inclination of the thoughts of his heart
was only evil all the time. The LORD was grieved that he had
made man on the earth, and his heart was filled with pain. So the
LORD said, "I will wipe mankind, whom I have created, from the
face of the earth—men and animals, and creatures that move
along the ground, and birds of the air—for I am grieved that I
have made them." But Noah found favor in the eyes of the LORD.
(Genesis 6:5-8)

God's judgment against the sin of people came in the form of a historical flood. The story goes that God spoke to the one man, Noah, and gave
him detailed instructions on how to build an ark (see Genesis 6:15-16).
Noah listened and obeyed. God saved Noah and his immediate family as
well as a boat full of animals. Through one man's faithfulness, a family
and an important element of creation were saved from the killing power
of the Flood.

The Flood story makes it clear that God's Word is at the center
of history. Noah trusted God for the unknown, and God kept his
word.

After the Flood, God made a covenant with people and his creation
that he would never again destroy all life with a flood (see Genesis 9:9-
17). The rainbow would be a sign of his promise.

As with Adam and Eve in the garden, God told Noah and his sons to
"be fruitful and increase in number; multiply on the earth and increase
upon it" (Genesis 9:7). The sons of Noah multiplied, but rather than
inhabiting the earth, they stayed localized. Genesis 11 describes how the
people had "one language and a common speech" and settled on a plain
in Shinar (verses 1-2):

Then they said, "Come, let us build ourselves a city, with a tower that reaches to the heavens, so that we may make a name for ourselves and not be scattered over the face of the whole earth."

But the LORD came down to see the city and the tower that the men were building. The LORD said, "If as one people speaking the same language they have begun to do this, then nothing they plan to do will be impossible for them. Come, let us go down and confuse their language so they will not understand each other."

So the LORD scattered them from there over all the earth, and they stopped building the city. That is why it was called Babel—because there the LORD confused the language of the whole world. From there the LORD scattered them over the face of the whole earth. (verses 4-9)

Sadly, the human family, even after a fresh start, was incapable of following God's relational Word. Foreshadowing secular humanism, their hearts were bent on the idea that living beings had tremendous worth apart from God. The direction of their hearts raced in the opposite direction of their Creator. Human unity replaced the fellowship of God, people, and place. They were satisfied to be known by one another rather than God, satisfied to walk with one another, not God. They sought human glory, fame, renown, authority, reputation, and achievement. All of this is the unspoken message behind the words, *Let us make a name for ourselves.* Once again, as with Adam and Eve, there was grace, and God acted on behalf of his creation to save them from themselves. God scattered the people, a move that led to all the racial and ethnic groups, all the nations of the world. Rather than destroy his creation, God chose to redeem people in the world.

The story of Noah and his family challenge the common misconception that the redemption Story is about God's saving individuals out of the world. That idea reduces salvation to personal escape from the evil physical world to a blissful spiritual heaven. In reality, redemption history is about an ongoing story and process where people are saved *in* the world. The way they are saved *out* of the world is by God's choosing them for himself, removing them out of the world's ways, giving them his ways, and then leaving them in the world to continue the work he has assigned them.

We're now into the third category in the larger controlling narrative: redemption. The redemption Story is about the history of the world and the creation of one nation set apart as God's people. (From this point forward, the Story begins to correspond with documented secular history, starting at about 2000 BC). This one nation will give birth to a new multinational community, though people won't understand this for quite some time. This people, whether the one nation or the community it gives birth to, is to be a model community of the one to come in the New Creation. This part of the story all begins with a man named Abram from the city of Ur (ironically, in what is modern-day Iraq).[1]

In Genesis 12:1-3, the Lord says to the man, Abram,

Leave your country, your people and your father's household and
go to the land I will show you.

I will make you into a great nation
    and I will bless you;
I will make your name great,
    and you will be a blessing.
I will bless those who bless you,
    and whoever curses you I will curse;
and all peoples on earth
    will be blessed through you.

At the heart of Jewish belief is the conviction that the one true God, who made the whole world, called Abraham and his family to belong to him in a special way (one man and a family). The promises God made to Abraham and his family, and the requirements that were laid on them, came to be seen in terms of the kind of agreement a king would make with his people or a husband and wife would make in marriage. Simply put, it was a covenant, a relationship between God and his people that included both promise and law.

In Genesis 17 the covenant was reaffirmed, and God gave Abraham instructions for keeping it: "This is my covenant with you and your descendants after you, the covenant you are to keep: Every male among you shall be circumcised. You are to undergo circumcision, and it will be the sign of the covenant between me and you" (verses 10-11).

Canon theologian N. T. Wright refers to circumcision as an "identity-marker." According to Wright, "With circumcision you knew where you were. A male was either circumcised or he wasn't. A man could no more be partly circumcised than a woman could be partly pregnant. It was a sure-fire test."[2]

Abraham was chosen so that he would "direct his children and his household after him to keep the way of the LORD by doing what is right and just, so that the LORD will bring about for Abraham what he has promised him" (Genesis 18:19). From this point forward in the Story, rightness and justice are a controlling theme.

The covenant with Abraham included (1) the promise of land, and (2) the promise that all people on earth would be blessed through him and his descendants. Just as with Noah, the earth (the land) figured into God's redemptive plans. God's promise to Abraham was the restoration of the Eden pattern of God, a people, and a land. As with Noah, through one man's faithfulness a family was saved. Only this time God expanded the idea of family to something massive, saying, "I will make your descendants as numerous as the stars in the sky and will give them all these lands, and through your offspring all nations on earth will be blessed" (Genesis 26:4).

Abraham was a friend of God, a man who believed God. Abraham was the type of human God seeks to be in relationship with. Like Noah, Abraham was a type of the new way to be human to come in Jesus. It is all of grace. It was God who moved to restore friendship with humankind. He chose Abraham, and beginning with one family he restored friendship with those called to believe his Word and to trust him for the unknown.

From Abraham and Sarah came Isaac and his son Jacob. Isaac married Rebekah, and Jacob married Rachel. Jacob also had Leah and a number of concubines. From Jacob and various mothers came the twelve tribes of Israel. They were named Israel because God renamed Jacob, Israel. He went from a name that meant "deceiver" to a name that meant "one who wrestles with God." God repeated to Jacob the Abrahamic promise of land, a multitude of descendants, and a kingly line (see Genesis 35:9-13).

Genesis really is a Book of Beginnings. It records the beginning of life and death, marriage, family, language, farming, technology, government, murder, adultery, rape, theft, and slavery. At the end of the Genesis story, we meet Joseph, son of Jacob (Israel). Joseph, sold into slavery by his own brothers, was taken to Egypt where he was sold a second time. Time passed, and in a God-appointed turnaround, Pharaoh put Joseph in charge of the whole land of Egypt. Eventually Joseph's family left Canaan for Egypt, and for four hundred years, things went well for Israel. Too well for Egypt's tastes though. Egypt said enough is enough and made slaves of the Israelites.

Next the infamous Moses entered onto the stage. The book of Exodus records the story of God's rescue of Israel from slavery and the agreement made between God and Israel at Mount Sinai where God spoke to Moses out of the burning bush.

God had heard the Israelites' cry for help and told Moses he'd seen their misery and was concerned for their suffering at the hands of the Egyptians.

> God said to Moses, "I AM WHO I AM. This is what you are to say to the Israelites: 'I AM has sent me to you.'"
>
> God also said to Moses, "Say to the Israelites, 'The LORD, the God of your fathers—the God of Abraham, the God of Isaac and the God of Jacob—has sent me to you.' This is my name forever, the name by which I am to be remembered from generation to generation." (Exodus 3:14-15)

So Moses asked the Egyptian pharaoh to let his people go free. Each time it appeared that Pharaoh would, he reneged. With each hesitation, God brought a nasty plague upon Egypt. The last one was more severe than all the others: The firstborn of every household would die. In order to save Israel from this suffering, God told Moses that he would pass over any household where the blood of a lamb was spread on the doorframe of the house. This last plague was too much, and Pharaoh relented. Israel left Egypt free, loaded down with the plunder of silver and gold.

This event became a powerful memory to be celebrated during Passover and other festivals. It added to the shape of Israel's faith in Yahweh (YHWH), seeing him as both Creator and Redeemer. Israel understood their redemption as freedom from four types of enslavement, what Old Testament scholar Christopher J. H. Wright categorizes as:

1. Political freedom—free from oppression.
2. Social freedom—free from interference in the family and way of life.
3. Economic freedom—free from slavery (labor).
4. Spiritual freedom—free from foreign gods and hindrance to worship.[3]

This "free" people—led by God in a pillar of cloud and fire—wandered, stumbled, and grumbled in the wilderness for forty years. Early on in the Israelites' wandering, Moses led them to Mount Sinai. There God gave Moses his personal word and will for Israel—the Ten Commandments and more.

Notice the pattern with God. He is speaking and acting, acting and speaking. God is personally involved with his people in a Word-and-work way, and he always has a human representative. First Adam, then man and woman together, then Noah, Abraham, and Moses (and Aaron). Moses, like the others, was a man who knew his Father's business. He had personal knowledge of God and God's agenda. He didn't obtain this through an intolerance of mystery, like Eve, but through hearing God speak and act. Moses listened and watched, then spoke and acted as God told him to.

The giving of the Law at Mount Sinai is recorded in Exodus 20–24. With the Law, Christopher J. H. Wright observed, "God began to mould for himself his own people. They would be a priesthood—a model people called out from among the nations, for the sake of the nations, to be a light to the nations as the vehicle and paradigm of God's redemption (cf. Exodus 19:4-6)."[4]

God began his personal Law by personal storytelling. In the prologue to the Decalogue, he recapped the Story: "I am the LORD your God, who brought you out of Egypt, out of the land of slavery" (Exodus 20:2). God communicated, "I am here, present in your life, sustaining you and caring for you. Here is the direction of life. Respond."

The Ten Commandments were Law and Covenant. They were a controlling story.

> When Moses went and told the people all the LORD's words and
> laws, they responded with one voice, "Everything the LORD has said
> we will do." Moses then wrote down everything the LORD had said.

He got up early the next morning and built an altar at the foot
of the mountain and set up twelve stone pillars representing the
twelve tribes of Israel. Then he sent young Israelite men, and they
offered burnt offerings and sacrificed young bulls as fellowship offerings to the LORD. Moses took half of the blood and put it in bowls,
and the other half he sprinkled on the altar. Then he took the Book
of the Covenant and read it to the people. They responded, "We
will do everything the LORD has said; we will obey."

Moses then took the blood, sprinkled it on the people and
said, "This is the blood of the covenant that the LORD has made
with you in accordance with all these words." (Exodus 24:3-8)

The descendants of one man, Aaron (Moses's brother), were chosen
to be priests, to serve in the Tent of Meeting which served as a tabernacle,
a sign of God's presence and protection. Their ordination and anointing
would continue for all generations to come.

In the outer courtyard was where sacrifices were made. This served as
a powerful memory maker, a reminder that the consequence of sin was
death. Sacrifices were required to remove the penalty of sin and disobedience. Innocent blood is shed for the guilty. This is what is known as substitutionary atonement, where a substitute suffers the judgment the sinner
deserves.

The many additional laws of Exodus 21 are the beginning shapes of
justice and mercy. They act as teachers, revealing to the Israelites that holiness is a better way of life. For hardened hearts, they crack the door to imitation of God. They are the seeds of restoration of the image of God in
humankind.

God's words and actions are ways of being and doing, but imitation alone
is not wholeness. Obedience is deeply connected to a response of grati-

tude. Loving gratitude is the sustaining, relational motive for obedient following. This idea will continue to be fleshed out more as the biblical Story unfolds. In summation it is: *What God has done for you, now do for others.* Obeying God's Law is relational. Obedience to it sustains relationship with God, other humans, and the planet. Obedience is wholly practical. It's love in practice.

For example, look at Exodus 23:9: "Do not oppress an alien; you yourselves know how it feels to be aliens, because you were aliens in Egypt." There's a principle at work that Israel needed then and we need today: *Don't forget what God has done for you.* In Creation, God gave the human family every provision needed for life, meaningful work, and unbroken relationship with himself, each other, and the earth. At the Fall, God chose to redeem rather than completely destroy. God kept speaking and acting on behalf of creation, on behalf of man and woman, his image bearers. He called a people to himself and promised that they would be a nation and that he would give them a land. God heard the cries of his people. He rescued them from slavery. He spoke and acted.

The history of God and people should motivate the continuing history of God and people. The Story is the fuel that drives the engine of following in obedience. This is why it's so dangerous for professing Christians to be disconnected from the historical drama Jesus took seriously. God calls his people *to step into the Story,* to look back, and in faith, step forward in time to make new history—to become contributing characters and narrators. If we see salvation as a personal story only, we will fail in our contribution to history. How? When we do step into a story it won't be the huge one we've been looking at in the last three chapters. The story we step into will be our own little one—one star in the sky, one grain of sand—not the whole Milky Way promise, but a nanosliver of it. What you want is the Story of the God of Abraham, Isaac, and Jacob—and nothing less.

After the death of Moses under the leadership of Joshua, the Israelites crossed the Jordan River and entered into the Promised Land, the land of Canaan, which they eventually conquered and claimed. This was a promise fulfilled for sure, but not yet the fulfillment of the larger promise God had in mind when he befriended Abraham.

The remaining books of the Old Testament give different shades and hues of Israel's story of God, people, and place. God continued to speak, giving his people further law, ritual, and specific instructions on worship (see Leviticus 26:1-13). As always, God expected obedience to his Word. The book of Numbers is a recap of Israel on the road from Mount Sinai to the boundary of Canaan. Deuteronomy, or the Second Law, is a review of the Law and a call to remember God. The stories of judges, prophets, priests, and kings continue in other books.

In the Old Testament story you see how the people of God were to be people of long memory. This holds for today as well. We are remember-ers, storytellers. Out of memory we do things. We celebrate memory, and we make memory in order to continue to tell the Story through word and work in our day-to-day lives.

It is this remembered Story that the Messiah Jesus stepped into.

The Opportunity for a New Way

When the time was right, the one true God sent his Son, Jesus, born of a woman "to be the Savior of the world" (1 John 4:14). God gave Jesus the authority to give personal, intimate knowledge of God to people. The way Jesus did this was to speak the Word of God and to be the Word made flesh (to embody the Word). People who encountered Jesus experienced personal, intimate knowledge of God. As Jesus said: "Anyone who has seen me has seen the Father" (John 14:9). Jesus was continuing the Story begun long ago.

In the Story line of redemption, the cross and the resurrection of Jesus are climactic historical events. Jesus, through these events, is God's victory over sin, evil, and the effects of the Fall. The victory is final. Student-followers of Jesus don't strive to achieve it. Their mission is to apply it to all of life—the total scope of life that sin has corrupted.

The death of Jesus is the death of a defiled Priest, one hung on a cross (tree) outside the city. God abandoned and sacrificed his own Son, so that through his shed blood, people could be forgiven their sins. Now they could return from exile in the world to a new, unceasing life of freedom in Messiah Jesus.

Following Easter and the resurrection of Jesus, the Story moves forward to Pentecost and the genesis of the church. The new chosen community of people belonging to God is birthed with Spirit-led direction and power. The same God direction and power that people saw and heard in Jesus is now found in his student-followers. They are kingdom people.

What is true of the King is now true of them. They have repented, stepped into the Story, and put their faith in the Word of God to tell them true stories about what it means to be human—what it means to be interested in the same things God is interested in. Now, in Jesus, all their senses are alive again.

~

Not long after I began to follow Jesus, I was booked to perform at Beaverbrook's, a club in Sacramento, California. As a matter of habit, I've always used the rest room right before going on stage, and that evening was no different. Standing there as men do, I read the graffiti. This was back before a more generous religious pluralism had seeped into people's hearts. On the wall before me was the indelible announcement: *Charlie Peacock has become a f***ing Christian!* Since this was America and not Ireland, I knew the writer wasn't happy.

Walking out of that rest room I felt like I was eight years old again, standing on the playground at Bridge Street School, having intercepted a note passed between tiny thugs who had written unmentionable cruelties with mangled grammar and crude penmanship. I felt like a man with a price on his head, and that somewhere out there in the dark night was a knife or a bullet waiting to escort me out of this world, sooner rather than later. Mostly, I felt alone and misunderstood.

When you're standing right smack in the middle of the scary moment, it's hard to think clearly. With a little distance you can make the connection between following Jesus and suffering. Memory kicks in. You remember that the light shines in the darkness, but the darkness doesn't understand what's happening (see John 1:15). You remember that Jesus was in the world, and even though everything was made through him, the world didn't recognize him. With a little memory and some space in between, you remember that the kingdom of God coming to earth is a real threat to all kinds of human economies and ways of being and doing. The threatened acting out of fear, flee or fight—sometimes with a black Sharpie on a bathroom wall.

It should be impossible, in fact, to talk about Jesus, the certain Word, without talking about the kingdom of God coming to earth. Talk of the kingdom is where Jesus began his own public conversation. " 'The time has come,' he said. 'The kingdom of God is near. Repent and believe the good news!' " (Mark 1:15). Dallas Willard's translation of Mark 1:15 cracks open the words for people not schooled in the lingo: Jesus says, "All the preliminaries have been taken care of and the rule of God is accessible to everyone. Review your plans for living and base your life on this remarkable new opportunity."[1]

I've always loved how David Wilcox's song "Show the Way" reveals the upside-down, almost subversive nature of the way the new opportunity is unfolding.

Look, if someone wrote a play
Just to glorify what's stronger than hate
Would they not arrange the stage
To look as if the hero came too late
As if he's almost in defeat
So it's looking like the evil side will win
So on the edge of every seat
From the moment that the whole thing begins
It is love who mixed the mortar
And it's love who stacked these stones
And it's love that made the stage here
Though it looks like we're alone
In this scene set in shadows
Like the night is here to stay

There is evil cast around us
But it's love that wrote the play
So in this darkness
Love can show the way[2]

The Word who wrote the play stepped out of heaven onto the earthly stage of his own creation. He did it to show the new way and to reveal the new opportunity to the human family, to bring life and light to those who would follow him out of the darkness.

His light was and is approachable light—each beam of brightness an invitation to follow. What Dallas Willard calls "the remarkable new opportunity" is the gospel or good news. The gospel is always about God's victory over evil and the rescue of his people. It gave first-century followers a simple one-word answer to what God was up to through Jesus.

Everyone who received Jesus and believed his gospel Story was given a new right: access to God. Because they were now with Jesus and not on their own, they could say, "We are children of God!" Everyone who followed Jesus heard him say in different ways and words, "This is the factual Story of God-people-and-place—this is where history was and is and where it's going. And this is what it means to be my student and follower—this is what it means to be interested in the same things God is interested in."

Concerning the factual story, Lesslie Newbigin writes that if it "were a fact that the one who designed the whole cosmic and human story has told us what the purpose is, then the situation would be different. That would be a fact of supreme and decisive importance."[3]

This is exactly what Jesus claimed for himself. In no uncertain terms, he stepped onto the stage as a historical fact of supreme and decisive importance, carrying with him other facts of supreme and decisive importance and saying things like, "I am the way and the truth and the life. No one comes to the Father except through me" (John 14:6). He clearly understood his purpose and the purpose of those he called as followers.

He came to destroy death and bring life and immortality into the view of all people at all times, so that everyone in every era would have a well-lit view of the remarkable new kingdom opportunity. Jesus brought all things in heaven and on earth together under one head and invited people to become active participants in the kingdom of God. Amazingly, this gift had been stored up in the heart of God, waiting for people since before the beginning of time. When the time to unveil it arrived, Jesus came telling his good news Story.

As it was in the first century, so it is today. Everyone who receives the gift is a gifted participant. What Christians call the church in the world is nothing less than all the gifted ones living and gathering as communities of kingdom people. Long before it's an institution, though, every church is meant to be a collective embodiment of the new way to be human—living in a right, free, and confident relationship with God, each other, and the creation. Together, followers are like living stones God is using to build a spiritual house—a house not made with hands.

The new way to be human begins with hearing and seeing. Followers of Jesus listen to his public conversation, his factual story. They see his very public, storied living. With word and work he tells his students, "This is the direction of life, this is the script, this is the defining story—essentially, these are the facts of life." As the descriptions make obvious, a follower follows a leader and a student learns from a teacher. Student-followers of Jesus *do base their lives* on the new opportunity their relationship with the Teacher-Leader offers. They form their personal interests according to what the Teacher-Leader is interested in.

The kingdom Jesus came announcing "created a new world, a new context, and he was challenging his hearers to become the new people that this new context demanded, the citizens of this new world."[4] This speaks to the subversive nature of the kingdom. The kingdom subverts darkness, replacing it with light. It replaces old anti-Artist ways of being human with the new way of Jesus. Technically speaking, the kingdom is God's sovereign and saving reign and rule. The rule being God's relational Word, his will. His reign or kingship is most evident when the interests of the King become the interests of the people, when individuals and communities faithfully live out what it means to follow Jesus. The kingdom is wherever and whenever the way of Jesus transforms people, place, and all ways of being, knowing, and doing.

~———

I still remember how the kingdom transformed my life from the moment I heard the good news and began to follow Jesus, how it challenged me to become the new citizen that the new context and opportunity demanded. Back then I was an artist who played mostly in Sacramento and Bay Area nightclubs. For extra income I also booked bands to play in three Sacramento clubs. Because my own band usually enjoyed standing-room-only crowds, I received 100 percent of the door and 10 percent of the bar. When I started seeing the kingdom for what it was, I remember telling the manager of Harry's Bar and Grill, "I can't accept 10 percent of the bar anymore." I'd been playing in clubs since I was sixteen years old. I knew exactly what the function of alcohol was in that setting, and it wasn't wine with dinner. I couldn't control how people behaved, but I could refuse to profit from their foolishness and the harm alcohol abuse might cause them and others.

In those days I had acquired a habit of using obscene and coarse language. Our tribe didn't give it much thought; it was just the way we talked. Of course, many of those same words, filled with venom, were used behind closed doors to hurt one another, to express hatred. I remember sitting in the back bedroom of our home, near the piano, reading Ephesians 5:4: "Nor should there be obscenity, foolish talk or coarse joking, which are out of place, but rather thanksgiving." And James 3:10: "Out of the same mouth come praise and cursing. My brothers, this should not be." *No, it shouldn't,* I thought. From that point on, how I talked and what I said was under kingdom rule. Because I now had access to God and was gaining personal knowledge of his ways of knowing, being, and doing, I naturally had to review my plans for living. So whether it was making money at Harry's Bar or talking in a particular way, everything would have to be based on the remarkable new opportunity. The kingdom subverted my plans for living, and in every instance God's ways were better. Still are.

Kingdom ideas are closely linked to the reality of Messiah. The word *Messiah* is Hebrew in origin, meaning "anointed one." In the Greek it translates as "Christos." If we say "Jesus Christ," we are stating "Jesus, the anointed one" (a title or description along with a proper name). With respect to what Jews at the time expected of the Messiah, the short version is this: Messiah is the King who is the true heir of David, the one whom YHWH (God) would use to rescue Israel from its enemies, to bring peace and rightness to the people of God. In a good kingdom, the king represents his people and the people represent the king. This is exactly what God had in mind with the coming of Messiah Jesus. King Jesus came representing the new way to be human to the human family.

To call followers of Jesus "Christians" is to call them "Messiah people," a name front-loaded with story. Messiah people are people of a historical climax and new identity resulting from the work of Messiah and the new opportunity he created for people to be reconciled to God. Messiah people is a unique description tied to a one-time-only event in history: the coming of Messiah. In the same way Messiah Jesus came representing the new way, his followers are called to represent the new way to the world.

For first-century Jews, the announcement of a kingdom with a David-type king would have been remarkably good news. The dreams and desires of Israel were invested in this kind of future hope. Even skeptics would have been curious. If true, the presence of such a kingdom would mean that the exile of the people of God had ended. The dream of the presence of God, with his people in his place, the holy city, would soon be a reality.

The story goes that the Israelites viewed exile as the result of their sin, and with good reason. The book of Deuteronomy served as a marker of long memory for the people of Israel. Chapters 29 and 30 had warned the people that if they broke their covenant with YHWH (God), he would send them into exile. They broke it, and God kept his word. Once again the people were scattered, homeless, oppressed, and enslaved.

This was not the end though. God told them, "When you and your children return to the LORD your God and obey him with all your heart and with all your soul according to everything I command you today, then the LORD your God will restore your fortunes and have compassion on you and gather you again from all the nations where he scattered you" (Deuteronomy 30:2-3). Israel looked for that day when God would speak with tenderness, saying "that her sin has been paid for, that she has received from the LORD's hand double for all her sins" (Isaiah 40:2).

God sent Jesus to be the relentless tenderness Israel had been hoping for. Jesus in the past, speaking through the prophet Isaiah, had told Israel:

I, even I, am he who blots out
    your transgressions, for my own sake,
    and remembers your sins no more. (Isaiah 43:25)

Listen to me, O house of Jacob,
    all you who remain of the house of Israel,
you whom I have upheld since you were conceived,
    and have carried since your birth.
Even to your old age and gray hairs
    I am he, I am he who will sustain you.
I have made you and I will carry you;
    I will sustain you and I will rescue you. (Isaiah 46:3-4)

Listen to me, O Jacob,
    Israel, whom I have called:

I am he;

    I am the first and I am the last.

My own hand laid the foundations of the earth,

    and my right hand spread out the heavens;

when I summon them,

    they all stand up together. (Isaiah 48:12-13)

The gospel of John speaks of Jesus, the certain Word, in this way: "In the beginning was the Word, and the Word was with God, and the Word was God. He was with God in the beginning. Through him all things were made; without him nothing was made that has been made. In him was life, and that life was the light of men" (John 1:1-4).

In Revelation 22:13, Jesus testifies, saying, "I am the Alpha and the Omega, the First and the Last, the Beginning and the End."

From beginning to end, there is the shadow or presence of Jesus in the Story. His identity is so full it moves from Creator to Prophet, Priest, and King. He's there in the beginning of Creation, and he's there to blot out sin and rescue his people. In the first century he announced that the kingdom was here, in this world. By ushering in the kingdom, Jesus initiated a new way to be human and called into being a renewed and greatly expanded Israel of God—not one nation delivered from exile, but a whole new nation delivered, one composed of people from every nation, language, and people group. The new opportunity of the kingdom way was to participate in all things new. As Revelation 21:5 says, "He who was seated on the throne said, 'I am making everything new!' Then he said, 'Write this down, for these words are trustworthy and true.'"

If my wife and I had not trusted that God was indeed making all things new, I don't know how we would have survived each other. Our life before following Jesus was so anti-Artist and antihuman that we had a mountain of sin to forgive. We would learn at the pace of toddlers that the inauguration of the kingdom brought with it a bigger sin-forgiveness than we could imagine. This was not just Jesus forgiving and taking away sin, it was his followers forgiving those who had sinned against them too. To refuse to forgive each other would be to refuse to be human in the new way. It would be like refusing to enter the gates of the kingdom. On many, many days we wanted to give up. It was just too hard. The weight of living with sin's pain felt eternally inescapable. We prayed for a welcoming countenance and disposition toward each other. We asked to be people equipped by the Spirit to offer forgiveness and acceptance on a radical and astonishing level. We knew then, in part, what we know now more clearly. God's forgiveness in us, working through us and for us, was and is our only hope of staying married. In ushering in the kingdom, Jesus brought healing and blessing to a broken people in a broken land. As individuals and as a couple, we are a part of the kingdom, healing and blessing.

When Jesus called people to repent, he was telling them to turn back and return to God. Israel understood this turning back primarily in two ways: (1) turning back from personal sin, such as David in Psalm 51, and (2) turning back as the only appropriate corporate response to God's kindness, such as when the Lord in Deuteronomy 30 told Israel he would have compassion on them if they returned to him and obeyed his Word.

Either way, corporate or personal, when Jesus called people to repent, he was telling them to give up their understanding of life and discover what it really meant to be human (after his own pattern), to be salty salt and bright light in the world. Regarding repentance, N. T. Wright says that "Jesus was summoning his hearers to give up their whole way of life, their national and social agendas, and to trust him for a different agenda, a different set of goals. This of course included a change of heart, but went far beyond it."[5]

The "far beyond it" that Wright alludes to is God's agenda to re-create for himself all of creation, including a multinational tribe who lives as his kingdom people. This is why salvation is not just personal. Salvation is the saving, re-creation work that God is doing with all his people and creation. That said, it's still important to address sin and repentance on a personal level. Of course, repentance means to turn from sin. Turning from sin's empty way of life to the fullness of life in God is foundational. Unrepentant and unforgiven sin keeps people unreconciled with God. If people remain unreconciled with God, if they refuse to live by his relational Word and to follow the Word made flesh, it is impossible for them to be truly human.

We know that sin has made a wreck of us all and that "all have sinned and fall short of the glory of God" (Romans 3:23). We also know from the Story that "the wages of sin is death, but the gift of God is eternal life in Christ Jesus our Lord" (Romans 6:23). To be or not to be is still the question. Sin equals death; the gift of God equals life. If I desire life, I must receive the gift God wants to give: Jesus and his perfect rightness and the new kingdom opportunity. As Acts 4:12 says, "Salvation is found in no one else, for there is no other name under heaven given to men by which we must be saved." It's by grace through faith in Jesus that anyone is saved. People cannot save themselves. They must accept the gift of God (see Ephesians 2:8).

The saving work of Jesus is finished. His victory over sin and death is one of cosmic proportions. Never again do sin and rebellion need to be dealt with in this way. Jesus has provided people with complete access to their Creator, complete atonement, and a clear conscience. He has inaugurated the kingdom rule of the King in the hearts of people and the creation itself. Everyone who receives the invitation to community with God and answers it by saying, "Thank you, count me in," becomes an unceasing participant in the Story of God-people-and-place.

~~~

Somewhere I picked up this idea regarding salvation. I think it's a good way of looking at it: We are saved from missing out on the good summation of the Story, and we are saved into the ongoing return of health in every sphere of life. There is no remarkable new opportunity without God's saving us, and we cannot become healthy co-conspirators in the Story without his help either. It's all of grace, all a gift.

When I was younger I got the idea that repentance was fessing up to particular sins, renouncing them, asking forgiveness for them, and turning from those particular sins toward right behavior. I even went through a dismal period where I made promises to God to never do the bad things again, or at least to try a lot harder not to do them. Without denigrating my good response of confessing sin or saying no to ungodliness, let me make clear that repentance is much more than simply fessing up to various sins or trying to do better. Since sin is always about having some other agenda than God's, repentance is first about turning from my false understanding of reality to God's true reality. When the eyes of my heart are enlightened, I see reality as it is and remark to myself, *Uh-oh, I'm moving in the wrong direction, away from God and his ways.*

If pressed to define *repentance* I would say: Repentance means giving up my way of living life and being human in exchange for the way God means his people to live life and be human. I've come to believe that God has a far better overall agenda for life than the one I've been following—one that includes the totality of existence. I'm not just sorry for thinking I had a better agenda, I'm sick over it. I'm so grateful that Wisdom has forgiven my arrogance and mistrust. Now I'm taking my cues, my script, from Jesus, the representative human. Through the revealed Word of the Bible, I watch Jesus speak and act. I hear his Word and watch him work. According to God's promise, I'm being made new in the likeness of Jesus. His way of being human is becoming mine. He's remaking my understanding of everything in life from sexuality, work, and friendships to the nature of life beyond my time on this earth.

As this happens, the eyes of my heart do become enlightened or spiritually informed. Paul prayed for this kind of enlightenment in Ephesians

1:18. When enlightenment comes, we see what God has done on behalf of all that he loves, ourselves included. Gratitude arrives, for it is God's kindness that leads us to repent, to make the exchange: We get the greatness of the kingdom agenda for letting go of our selfish worldly agenda. Transformation is a long, slow burn, and we begin to live in response to this ever-transforming reality. This is how and why I gave up the 10 percent from the bar and the language of my previous tribe. Student-followers pattern the shape of our responses after the new way to be human that Jesus shows us. But we are never alone in this. We are cooperating with what God has promised to do. Jesus fulfilled the Law, the rightness of God for us, and is now fulfilling the Law in us, making us, step by step, this new way to be human. Every good word and work comes from God, "For we are God's workmanship, created in Christ Jesus to do good works, which God prepared in advance for us to do" (Ephesians 2:10).

The Word and Work of Jesus

Jesus was walking along the Sea of Galilee when he came across two fishermen brothers, Peter and Andrew. They would become his first student-followers. He said to the brothers, "Come, follow me...and I will make you fishers of men" (Mark 1:17). Without hesitating Peter and Andrew left their nets and followed Jesus.

This is how the calling to Jesus, for Jesus, works. Jesus speaks to people. He offers an invitation to walk with him on a journey. This is the calling. Second, there is an exchange. Jesus makes a confident promise (his relational, covenant Word) to those who accept his invitation to follow. He promises to transform work. He gives his followers a new and better overarching vocation, one guided by him. He provides his followers with new tools, the net for drawing people to himself and his ways of being human.

~~~

Following Jesus requires faith and repentance. Peter and Andrew responded without hesitation. They dropped their agenda for God's (for the moment at least).

Following Jesus (then and now) changes the shape of family, of community—from family of man to the family of God. This is another reason why personal salvation is too small a controlling story. Peter and Andrew did not "get saved" and retreat to a vacation fishing village. They become players in the fulfillment of God's covenant with Abraham. Every follower of Jesus plays this role in history to some degree.

In the story of the disciples' calling, there's a pattern worth taking note of. God speaks; God promises. Through Jesus, God sent a perfectly faithful, direct representative to call a multitude of representatives to himself, people who would walk with him forever. It's through one man, Jesus, that a multitude "as numerous as the stars in the sky and as the sand on the seashore" will come (Genesis 22:17).

Next in the story, Jesus called James and John, and they also left their boat, nets, and father to follow Jesus.

The first followers realized, saw, and heard that:

1. They were not unique, except in being first. People will accept the invitation to follow, and two will become four, four will become eight, and so on. This is the pattern of God's calling a people to himself through one faithful man, his Son. Jesus fulfilled the earlier Genesis mandate "be fruitful and multiply" in a brand-new way.

2. Their vocation, their family would change overnight simply by following Jesus (by walking with God), and they would be all right. A new way of being, of living would emerge step by step.

3. They were student-followers being taught and led. They did not choose their Teacher-Leader, he chose them. Here again, God is personal, acting on behalf of his creation. His word is relational and invitational. It's quite different from the modern construction of asking people if they know Jesus as their personal savior.

We see a clear Jesus-model for making fishers of men. It's not efficient or easy though, and this may be why it's used so infrequently. Jesus showed his followers that the way to be human involves word and work patterned after his own. His Word is speaking and telling. His work is acting and showing. One is storytelling, the other storied living. Jesus explained the story and announced the certainty of the kingdom. He embodied the kingdom through the work of healing and serving. His Word and his works told stories in their own way.

Word and work go together in an inseparable fashion, just as they have from the beginning. This is the relational and creational Word of God brought forward in time and embodied in the Word made flesh. It's this combination of storytelling and storied living that draws people to Jesus.

This way of being human after the pattern of Jesus is the new tool, the new net, the new overarching vocation Jesus promised to give to those who follow him. It's a magnetic and attractive way of being. In Jesus it amazed, surprised, and caused people to feel wonder. The word and work of his followers should invite this same kind of reaction today. It should do now as it did then: cause people to say God *is,* and to declare his excellence. The chart on pages 74 and 75 helps me visualize the mission.

After Jesus showed his followers the way through Word and work, he sent them out as his direct representatives saying, "All authority in heaven and on earth has been given to me. Therefore go and make disciples of all nations, baptizing them in the name of the Father and of the Son and of the Holy Spirit, and teaching them to obey everything I have commanded you. And surely I am with you always, to the very end of the age" (Matthew 28:18-20).

He blessed them, saying, "Peace be with you! As the Father has sent me, I am sending you" (John 20:21).

—————

Recently I was eating breakfast at a little diner in Estes Park, Colorado. A sign in the window read: "This life is a test. It is only a test. If this had been a Real Life, you would have received further instructions as to where to go and what to do." Apparently the writer of this folksy aphorism was unfamiliar with Jesus. The eternal life of an unceasing follower of Jesus begins the moment you step into the Story as an active participant. For a student-follower, eternal life has already begun. This life is not a test run or a rehearsal.

In John 17:1-26, Jesus gave plenty of instruction and defined eternal life in a way quite different from the average chatter on the subject. Verse 3 is most specific: "Now this is eternal life: that they may know you, the only true God, and Jesus Christ, whom you have sent." In the entire chapter 17 text, there is no mention of a place such as heaven or mansions of glory. According to Jesus, eternal life is about epistemology before it is about eschatology. It is about knowing before it is about going. You could also say that it is eschatology defined by epistemology. In other words, one's future life is determined by whether one knows God, specifically Messiah Jesus who was sent to earth by God.

Jesus gives the human family his own personal knowledge of the way things are—past, present, and future. If any human wants eternal life, life without end, full and complete, lacking nothing, he or she must begin with intimate knowledge of God. This knowledge is made up of:

1. *Personal knowledge through personal relationship*—the one true God sent Messiah Jesus to embody the relational Word and to reconcile all relationships, first among them the relationship between the Creator and his people.

2. *Personal knowledge of God's personal knowledge*—his agenda, his ways, his rule—revealed by him to his people through Word and work. The Father gave Jesus the authority to give personal intimate knowledge of God to people. The way Jesus did this was to both speak the word of the prophets and to be the Word, to embody it. Personal intimate knowledge of God was experienced by people as they encountered Jesus. Again, as Jesus said, "Anyone who has seen me has seen the Father" (John 14:9).

Galatians 2:20 tells me, "I have been crucified with Christ [Messiah] and I no longer live, but Christ [Messiah] lives in me. The life I live in the body, I live by faith in the Son of God, who loved me and gave himself for me."

The Jesus Model for Making Fishers of Men

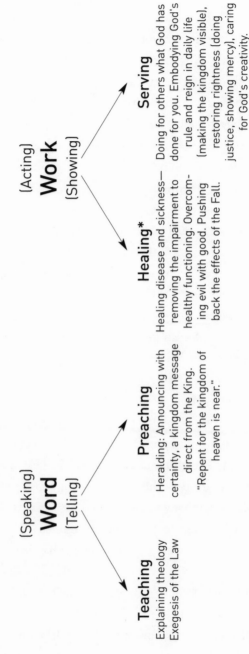

(Speaking)
Word
[Telling]

(Acting)
Work
[Showing]

Teaching
Explaining theology
Exegesis of the Law

Preaching
Heralding: Announcing with certainty, a kingdom message direct from the King. "Repent for the kingdom of heaven is near."

Healing*
Healing disease and sickness—removing the impairment to healthy functioning. Overcoming evil with good. Pushing back the effects of the Fall.

Serving
Doing for others what God has done for you. Embodying God's rule and reign in daily life (making the kingdom visible), restoring rightness (doing justice, showing mercy), caring for God's creativity.

Storytelling ─────────────→ Storied Living

Draws the People In

"Large crowds followed him..." Matthew 19:2

"The people were amazed at his teaching, because he taught them as one who had authority, not as the teachers of the law." Mark 1:22
After healing the paralytic: "This amazed everyone and they praised God, saying, 'We have never seen anything like this!'" Mark 2:12

Caused amazement: surprised, to feel with wonder.
Caused praise to God.

This is the why of worship!

Certainty: God, you are the Creator and re-Creator. You alone are worthy of worship.
People are compelled to speak and sing the certainties back to God. Many who are amazed praise God and continue the pattern of storytelling and storied living. They replicate word and work again and again.

*Regarding healing: Many alert Christians throughout history have picked up on this and made it integral to ministry. Unfortunately, most have failed to see healing as holistic in scope, affecting the whole person, the earth, and all enterprise. This is the healing that climaxes with the new heavens and new earth. When Jesus walked the earth, people were predisposed to seek healing. These healings were authentic and obviously needed. Nevertheless, they foreshadow "I am making everything new!" (Revelation 21:5).

Student-followers are called to live life in a whole new way, a way defined by the crucified and risen Messiah Jesus, with his life at work within us. If the old way to be human (the way that is against God's ways) has been crucified with Messiah, and Messiah now lives in me, what is true of Messiah ought to be true of me. Increasingly, I ought to live in response to this new identity (in cooperation with sanctification). I ought to live a life worthy of someone who professes to follow Jesus, to "please him in every way: bearing fruit in every good work, growing in the knowledge of God" (Colossians 1:10).

Messiah people are a community of invitation. It's God who has invited and gathered people together. Once gathered, the community of invitation becomes a community of response. Those who in faith trust the Messiah story, who say, "That looks like love to me," live true to the story, identity, and mission of Messiah Jesus. Christians (Messiah people) are the evidence that God's Word is true, that all his covenants (promises) are yes in Jesus the Messiah. "For no matter how many promises God has made, they are 'Yes' in Christ. And so through him the 'Amen' is spoken by us to the glory of God" (2 Corinthians 1:20).

Student-followers of Jesus have a new mark of identity. Israel, through promise (or covenant), was set apart as God's people, having the identity markers of circumcision and the Jewish Law. Now those who belong to the true Israel, Jesus, have a new identity and new identity markers, specifically faith in Jesus expressing itself through love. The identity of Israel, or the chosen ones, is no longer defined by the Law. As Paul said in Galatians, followers of Jesus have died to the Law that they might live for God (see Galatians 2:19).

God inaugurated through Jesus a New Creation and a new way of living. Even now we see glimpses of it wherever the reign and rule of King Jesus, the Messiah, is present. The good news is that Messiah Jesus has come, inviting all humans to follow him, to come and see, and to actively participate in his constantly arriving kingdom. This is news of ultimate importance because it makes claims about what reality actually is.

The new way to be human is a word-and-work mission defined and shaped by love of God and neighbor. All word and work is meant to obey Jesus's summation of the Law in Matthew 22:37-40. The essence of the new way to be human is: Do for others as Jesus has done for you; make the kingdom, the rule of God known and visible. A surefire test of whether you are following in the new way or not is this: Does it look like love expressing itself through word and work? There is no making of authentic student-followers of Jesus except after the pattern of the love-motivated word and work Jesus revealed.

Know the Story you profess to be participating in. Know it well and tell it with enthusiasm. Tell it like you tell other stories that excite and compel you. Learn to do this first before you memorize a load of verses disconnected from the whole. You can learn lots of individual verses later after you have the broader context of the Story. When you first learn to tell the Story, get the shape right. Then fill in the details. The shape of the Story is distinctive even in its basic form—just as the shape of a giraffe is distinct. An outline of a giraffe is clearly a giraffe and not a mouse. Learn to tell the Story clearly in its basic outline form.

We learn the explanatory Story in order to create more little stories that explain life to our family and neighbors. These stories are meant to be a show-and-tell testimony to the veracity of the main narrative. They are meant to be congruent with the new way to be human Jesus left us in charge of. As you go about the business of following Jesus, more will be revealed, and you'll incrementally fill in the details. It's good work and plenty of labor for the rest of your days.

The Personal Connection

One Small Story of a Love Supreme

Every human steps into the Story of God, people, and planet whether he or she acknowledges it or not. This is one of the certainties that student-followers of Jesus hold to. The difference for those who follow Jesus with intentionality is that they step into the faith that already exists within a people. They become active participants in the Story of God, *his people,* and his planet. They are the collective student-followers who have answered his invitation to follow in the new way to be human that Jesus inaugurated.

I, Charles William Ashworth, stepped into the Story of God-people-and-place from the womb of my mother, Alice Margaret Ashworth, previously Williamson. Global location: Yuba City, California—the first Fremont Hospital on Plumas Street, around the corner from Hal's Grubstake, home of the "Dude Burger" and a "Saddlebag of Fries." The story goes that seed and ovum with my name on them joined on a wintry December evening in Cheyenne, Wyoming, 1955. My father, Bill, was stationed in Cheyenne, called by Uncle Sam to play trumpet for the U.S. Air Force Band.

Bill was born in Oroville, California, to Lee Jackson Ashworth and Ella Nora Ashworth, previously Baggett. They named him Calvin Willard Ashworth, though the family called him Willie, and later, Bill. He never used Willard. When a middle name was necessary, he preferred to substitute William.

There's a history of liquidity in naming within my family. Here's three generations worth: I'm known as Charlie Peacock (a last name lifted from jazz bassist Gary Peacock). In addition to altering his middle name, my father would truncate his last name to Ash. In the early 1970s he played a long engagement at the Table Mountain Tavern as part of the Bill Ash Quartet, featuring Pete Baker on organ. To his deathbed, my grandfather Marvin Williamson argued that his middle name was Gentle, though the birth certificate shows proof of the equally odd, General.

The Ashworth tribe (along with the Baggetts) came west from Louisiana to work in lumber. As the name indicates, the Ashworths are a long line of woodworking people. My grandfather Lee had a bit of the drifter in him, which fit well with the transient logging and sawmill life. Story has it that the family's frequent movement may have been a holdover habit from the past, when Ashworths moved often due to persecution for their unusual racial mix, that of Redbones.[1]

Eventually, after living in several sawmill communities, the Ashworths planted themselves in Yuba City. It was there that my mother met the young trumpeter, Bill.

Alice was born in Durant, Oklahoma, to Marvin Gentle Williamson and Lois Williamson, previously Miller. The Williamson tribe came west to Yuba City in 1939 to find work and have a fresh go at life. Alice's maternal grandfather Robert Dallas Miller preceded them and found employment as a peach tree pruner and picker. He'd lined up fruit labor for the rest of the family too. After one day in the orchard, Alice's father, the Gentle General, told Grandpa Miller, "I didn't come all the way to California to pick no damn peaches."

As far back as my memory goes, Grandma and Grandpa Ashworth were followers of Jesus. Much later in life, Grandma Williamson began to follow Jesus with serious intent. She (and Marvin, too) attended St. Andrew's Presbyterian Church in Yuba City. I don't know exactly why I want to say this, but there's something really beautiful about an Okie Presbyterian.

Other memories of Christians and church come to me without much effort. My best friend Brad Barkley couldn't play on certain evenings after dinner because of family Bible reading and prayer (his mother, Lydia, was a follower). My feeling at the time was, What kind of God doesn't let kids play? It wasn't too long before I found out. My Ashworth grandparents, members of The First Christian Church in Marysville, arranged for my dad to be the new choir director. As it was, the choir needed another soprano, so Dad made me share his torture. Neither my father nor I followed Jesus. Dad was doing it for extra money. I had no such motivation and couldn't believe it was happening to me. Rehearsals were at five o'clock on Sunday evening, right during some of the best programming on television, the Abbott and Costello movie hour.

In 1972, I was fifteen years old, in love with Andi and music, and that's about all, except for the occasional thrill of dirt biking when the Honda would start. Along with pop and R&B, I listened to the best of jazz and improvisational music, including the great artist, John Coltrane. Late at night, alone in my room, I would light a candle and a little cone of incense, put Coltrane on the stereo, and invite him to transport me to new worlds of sound and invention. It was for me, as people often remarked in those days, a religious experience, and admittedly no small part of my attraction to Coltrane. I read everything I could about him in magazines, books, and liner notes. One writer explained Coltrane's premature death at the age of forty by postulating that a man cannot see God and live. The inference, even to my young mind, was understood and noted. John Coltrane was a very spiritual man, a deeply religious man. I was trying to be.

A year or so prior to discovering Coltrane, I had a more formal brush with Christian religion—more than singing in the choir. Due to a mysterious ailment, my mother was hospitalized for a time in San Francisco. She returned home to Yuba City a different person. She had experienced some kind of encounter with Messiah Jesus. What exactly, I don't recall. I do remember walking up the aisle of First Christian hand in hand with her, professing to the minister Don Roberts our desire to become Christians. A class for new believers preceded our baptism.

I attended youth group, brought Andi to church and Sunday school, read my Bible, sang in the choir, preached a "youth sermon" on God and people using a somewhat sketchy baseball analogy, told Andi and my parents I would be attending Bible college after high school (in order to become a minister), and then, to my surprise, the whole Christian thing ended as quickly as it began. Being a Christian wasn't working for me. I was starting to have problems with the exclusivity of its claims. Besides that, I was worn out from denying myself certain sexual pleasures that seemed to be deeply entwined with falling in love. There were other issues as well, not the least of them, John Coltrane.

Coltrane wrote songs with titles like "A Love Supreme," "Ascension," and "The Father and the Son and the Holy Ghost." He was spiritual, in touch with the Creator. I admired him and wanted to model my life after his. I had to wonder, would John Coltrane be received with open arms by the good Christians at my church? I figured no and started getting some extra sleep on Sundays.

I continued in my attempts to be spiritual like Coltrane and my poetry mentor, Gary Snyder. I thought spirituality would make me a disciplined musician, able and equipped to create at the highest level, like Coltrane. I continued to believe in God and Jesus, even that Jesus was the Savior. I had no beef with him. My problem was with what people called "organized religion."

~~~

A couple of years before Coltrane and my experience with my mom at The First Christian Church, I had a frightening and disturbing dream of murder. I was ten years old at the time and sick with mononucleosis. I dreamed that I had killed God.

According to R. C. Sproul, "God is our mortal enemy. He represents the highest possible threat to our sinful desires. No amount of persuasion by men or argumentation from philosophers or theologians can induce us to love God. We despise His very existence and would do anything in our power to rid the universe of his holy presence."[2]

Even murder him?

Sproul continues, "If God were to expose His life to our hands, He would not be safe for a second. We would not ignore Him; we would destroy Him."[3]

I suppose we would. People showed little or no hesitation in killing Jesus. Our hearts, it seems, are bent on getting God out of the picture. Some people attempt to achieve the goal by fighting for the notion that God simply does not exist—never has, never will. Others trumpet his death. This tactic can take the shape of a faux respectability similar to when a patriarch passes—God can be spoken well of, but serving him is no longer functionally necessary. Or, as with Nietzsche, God is dead because he was always a creation of the human imagination, and the human imagination has no more need of him. Other equally inventive people offer the idea that God is the impersonal force behind the universe. An impersonal god is a mute god, and a mute god is a god who does not speak—does not have a relational word. By designing a speechless god, we avoid relationship and accountability for being human. People can be quite inventive when looking for solutions to the problem of God and words.

Between the ages of fifteen and twenty-five, I did my part to rid the universe of God by maintaining belief in a personal God while living as if he were impersonal, nonrelational, or even nonexistent (depending on what suited me best). Second, I took false notions of the Tri-personal God of Christianity and, like tossing a salad, mixed them up with religions and philosophies that embraced Christ as a great teacher while, at the same time, sought to undermine his teachings. The effect of this contradictory, twofold approach rendered any semblance of the one true God null and void. I named God as God, but there was nothing behind the name. He existed like a phony passport. You could read his name, and it all looked official, but in reality no such person existed. This method allowed for talk of God and spirituality, but its effect was no less deadly. The name remained, but God was clearly out of the picture.

In a previous book, *At the Crossroads,* I told the story of my spiritual awakening, and how it began through a Twelve Step recovery group. I was twenty-five at the time and had already been married for seven years. When I first became part of the group, I was told to choose a higher power and turn my life over to it. If I didn't, they said I would never get clean and sober. Maybe it was the fact that I had taste tested so many religions and spiritualities by that time and found them wanting, or maybe it was socialization. Regardless, I reverted to a memory, an older controlling story. I chose the God of the Bible to be my higher power.

While no one can say for sure what God was affecting in my life at the beginning of my sobriety, one thing is certain: I did not pray to the God of the Bible out of love for him, his Word, or his agenda. I prayed out of desperation and self-preservation, betting that if the God of the Bible did in fact exist, he would be the necessary positive fix to counteract the negative influences that alcohol and drugs had become. Since all my attempts to fix myself had been unsuccessful, I had nothing to lose and everything to gain by giving the God of the Bible a chance at doing what I could not do for myself. I liked the idea of talking to God and trusting him with my life one day at a time.

What I didn't understand back then was that I was having a very one-sided conversation. I was talking to God, but he wasn't talking to me—except through the biblically congruent ideas embedded in the Twelve Step recovery literature. I gave him the seat of power but no tongue with which to speak. I had created a speechless God. I was a desperate man interested in practical results, not in following Jesus. Thankfully, the Artist who cares for what he loves had something else in mind.

In March of 1982 I took a single gig as a sub, playing piano for jazz saxophonist Michael Butera. Mike was a Christian of the born-again variety. I was determined not to hold it against him. After all, I had been praying to the God of the Bible for twelve months or so, asking for only a few things, really—sobriety and work. Both were coming, slow by slow, like the drip of a faucet. Perhaps the God of the Christians was alive and well, listening to the pleas of the foolish.

At the end of the gig, I thanked Mike for hiring me and communicated that I was grateful for the work. A month later I received a phone call from him. While Mike was praying, it seemed God had impressed upon him that he should contact me and ask if we could meet and pray together. Mike was very sensitive and respectful and didn't want to appear, as he said, "weird." Though it was an odd request, I tried my best to put him at ease.

"I pray all the time," I told him. "Come on over."

Within minutes Mike was at my door, and we headed to the back of the house. He'd come to tell me the Story of Jesus.

To tell the Story of Jesus, to ask someone to consider its truthfulness, is to say, "Picture this." And when truth interacts with an imagination supernaturally charged with faith, belief will announce itself. It always does. So it was with me.

Mike told me that there was something wrong with people and that the something had a name: sin. Sin, he told me, was alienating me from God, and until the sin problem was taken care of, I could never truthfully be in relationship with God even if I was talking to him every day.

With my imagination alive to truth and my need before me, I knew that Mike was right: Jesus was the Savior of the world—my Savior, too. What Mike was telling me seemed to explain reality better than any explanation I'd every heard. Time suddenly unwound to a stop, and I imagined a line separating two lives: the one I'd been living, and the one in Jesus that beckoned me. I was amazed and afraid. I knew that if I stepped over the line into life with Jesus, there would be no turning back. I would have to leave my old life behind. But what choice did I have? If I refused to cross over, I would knowingly be accepting a different story and an untruthful life. Having heard the best story but refusing to accept it, I would be the most miserable person in the world. Time came alive again, and I spoke aloud a life-defining prayer, confessing my need and requesting the kindness of God. Truth became my tears, and like the praying multitude before me, I believed. I trusted that God would deal with me according to his great compassion and promises. In faith I believed in Jesus as the certain, sinless Word and trusted him for the unknown, infinite road that now stretched out before me.

The genesis of new days and new nights had begun with prayer, and the future would be fueled by it as well. Talking with God became the same as blood and breath and water—essential and common. I learned that chattering with the Divine defines the life of someone who wants to be holy and creative. It is the big conversation. It is the ultimate what-if. I also learned that it's good to say thank you and I love you, to let my prayers morph into praise then cross-fade again into requests. All in all, I learned that there is life in prayer, a life as real and visceral and messy as any life you can know.

Now, twenty-plus years later, I see that praying is like putting on clothes in the morning. It covers my nakedness and answers the Edenic question, "Where are you, Chuck?" My prayers announce my location and my status—"Here I am God!"—dissolving any pretense that I am anything other than a small and needy man. This is the kind of effect Jesus has on people. It's all a part of his plan. He moves us from being the kind of people who use his creation to hide from him to being the kind of people who eagerly seek an authentic God-human conversation. This is exactly what Jesus came to earth to achieve.

So when we pray, our prayers are like sirens warning us of the presence and power of God. Here he comes, look out! The world is not the same as it was a nanosecond before. When God's will is done on earth as it is in heaven, the blind do see, the lame walk, and the captives are set free. The cancer inside a young mother will disappear, a defective engine will start, a marriage will be healed, an orphan will know a parent's love, a child will cease flirting with drugs, and an angel will come to the aid of some needy human here on planet Earth. And on some days, when it's really necessary, God will send a saxophonist with a long memory, carrying the words of life while riffing on "A Love Supreme."

The Bible tells me that even while I was still living the lifestyle of one who was against God's ways, he demonstrated his love for me through the death and resurrection of his Son, Jesus. Thank God, my saxophonist friend took this story seriously. How could he not? It had widened his view of reality to such a degree that he had no option but to invite others to find their own place in it as well. This kind of invitation is the word and work of all Messiah people—telling the story and inviting others to follow Jesus in the new way.

Following Jesus in the New Way

Knowing the story you're participating in will affect the kind of person you become. Children who have no sense of family history (good or bad) become different kinds of people than they would if they had a sense of participating in a story larger than their own. It is a product of our collective amnesia that children grow up thinking that life begins at their birth. It would be better for children to understand birth as the moment they step into the flow of the Story of God-people-and-place. The new birth Jesus spoke of changes a person's status in the Story, creating a new flow in a right and well-lit direction.

For student-followers, the new way is composed of doing what Jesus taught us to do. Jesus did nothing on his own, only what the Father told him. He was about his Father's business. He points his followers in this same well-lit direction, and then empowers them by the Spirit to stay the course.

A few years ago, at an important crossroad, I received a card from a friend. It was titled "Don't Look Back." The card depicted a person choosing one road over another. To the left was a road called "Your Life." To the right was a road called "No Longer an Option." This is the way it is for followers of Jesus. Don't look back. The old way of living life is no longer an option.

Religious people love the sound of God-thoughts colliding with their ears. They feel superior for having recognized accurate theology. I know I do.

What we don't love, treasure, and crave is to actually have the brightness of God's ways take over our lives. We like to keep our options open—play loose with God and words. What's the alternative to takeover? If I believe in God, yet reject a God-informed, God-directed life, what is the nature of my belief? Practically speaking, do I *believe* in a God whom I *believe* is unworthy of *belief*? If so, doesn't this contradiction expose me as a fool?

After all, how can I follow Jesus, walk with him, and not be changed? How can any of us who profess to be followers of Jesus follow him without embodying the answer to the question of what life in Messiah is? How can we say we are followers and not have the Father's business redirect and define our business?

Theologians write that many Christians profess belief but often believe in something other than the Story of God-people-earth-and-sky. What does this mean? Aren't Christians born-again, Spirit-filled believers—the only true believers? They are the ones who have wisely received Jesus Christ as their personal Savior. Correct? Their sins are forgiven. They are saved and going to heaven. They help others get saved. What evidence do these academic/theological types have to support the notion that many Christians believe in something other than the way of Jesus?

The truth is, they have the evidence of what professing Christians say and do. They have the stories. They can see that there's not enough light in the stories of the gathered tribe (the church) to inspire a mass of comprehensive models of what it means to be authentic, intentional followers of Jesus. When you do see one of these intentional followers, he or she really stands out. My friend Bob Briner was one.

Bob's work, particularly in his last years, was to give himself away for the sake of God's agenda in the world. For most of his professional life, he'd been involved in sports television. He was one of the best writer/ producers in the world and was instrumental in bringing the sport of tennis to the little screen. In the early nineties he started phasing out of sports broadcasting in order to have more time to write and give himself away. Bob, the author of ten books, left this place and went into the presence of Jesus on June 18, 1999. That same month I attended a planning session for a Bob Briner tribute and memorial service to be held in October at Spring Arbor College.

During that season I made an entry in my prayer journal, something I didn't want to forget:

> What if every Christian lived life in such a way that, upon their death, a tribute and memorial service had to be planned? I don't mean a funeral, I'm talking about a celebration where thousands are invited and story after story is told of how one human being gave himself away in the power and in the name of Jesus. If every student-follower lived with the intentionality that Bob did, this would be a very different world and critics of the church would have considerably less to say.

Frank Deford, respected writer and NPR commentator, spoke at the memorial service for Bob. He called Bob an angelic man, tough, practical, and witty. Frank told the audience that though he was one of the token sinners present to honor Bob, he knew that Bob Briner lived "the uncompromising Christian life that he wrote about, where love proceeds and care follows and generosity abounds."

Critics of Jesus-followers have a just basis for criticism if the fruit of our following looks more like the lives of the Pharisees and Sadducees than those overtaken by the love of God, such as the prostitute Mary, the tax man Matthew, and the murderer Paul. People should be skeptical when our version of the ongoing story looks more like a life of materialism, greed, self-absorption, and seeking peace and safety at any cost than a life of imitating and trusting Jesus in the new way. When it comes to criticism, followers often play right into the hands of those who disregard or question the trustworthiness of the Story. If God's people are wise, they will take the posture of the teachable sinner and search the criticism for any good thinking, any clear insights, any evidence of yes.

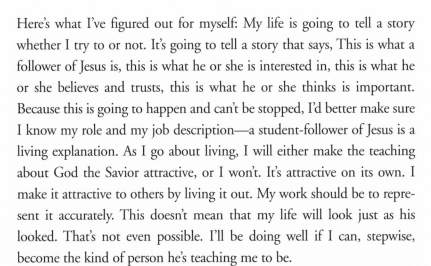

Here's what I've figured out for myself: My life is going to tell a story whether I try to or not. It's going to tell a story that says, This is what a follower of Jesus is, this is what he or she is interested in, this is what he or she believes and trusts, this is what he or she thinks is important. Because this is going to happen and can't be stopped, I'd better make sure I know my role and my job description—a student-follower of Jesus is a living explanation. As I go about living, I will either make the teaching about God the Savior attractive, or I won't. It's attractive on its own. I make it attractive to others by living it out. My work should be to represent it accurately. This doesn't mean that my life will look just as his looked. That's not even possible. I'll be doing well if I can, stepwise, become the kind of person he's teaching me to be.

I've decided my work is to step into the Story with intentionality and live a life framed and filled with God-thoughts about reality—what Jesus has said life is really about. My goal is not to be a born-again Christian, a good Christian, a religious fanatic, a do-gooder, a spiritual person, a nice guy, an American evangelical, or a good Catholic. My hope is that others will name me as an honest-to-God student-follower of Jesus, someone with a heart full of his brightness, following in the new way. It's not wise to name yourself as a Christian unless you are actually embodying the way of Messiah Jesus. If you are embodying the way, it will be as obvious as Jesus was obvious. If it is obvious, the necessity of naming yourself will fade. Others will do it for you. Questions may arise, and if so, you answer them. If people want to know why you head in one direction and not another, tell them who you're following.

It's unfortunate that many of us with the desire to follow go off-course and become suspect right from the start. Of course, our individual sin is to blame, but so are our teachers, those who model the way for us. Every young follower has human teachers—those among us who have authority and who through word and work seem to know something about following Jesus. Many people, myself included, claim to know something about Jesus and speak with confidence. I read about him in the Bible. I think, write, and speak about him. I speak with him in prayer, and I claim to follow him as a student follows a master-teacher. All of this is true of me. Yet the whole history of Christianity reveals that even the most sincere followers can misunderstand Jesus and his mission. Even the most committed have distorted the Jesus story to their own end.

It is a serious problem for young followers when the experienced followers they watch are busy at something other than what Jesus wants his people to be, know, speak, and do. This was one of the problems the East Tennessee Wilderness Prophet was talking about. The followers he was living in community with were confusing him. His whole being screamed out: *This can't possibly be the way of following…is it?* He was right to question and grieve if indeed they weren't living in the way.

What you learn by studying church history and by simply looking around you is that there are many ways to create the appearance of following that are no more than surface games of little depth and no mystery. Expose them, and all you find is contemporary, popular Christian culture. It is basically consumer religion co-opting language from the Story. It is not necessarily the good Story itself. It's not the tribal knowledge of the Israel of God, people of the new way to be human. No one should be satisfied with anything less.

Some older followers veer from the new way via the sickness of amnesia. We forget the Story and the way of Jesus. When any follower loses connection to reality, his or her embodied life becomes deservedly suspect. There's no longer any distinction between a life of following Jesus and a life of not following. There's no contrast. No art. And art is always present where God is.

I know this insanity well. I run to cheap substitutes, lies, and sneaky roads. I forget what I know to be true. People are right to criticize me. I am suspect. Because I am, I pray daily for the redirect of God and the takeover of Jesus. *Spirit,* I pray, *come flush the lies out.*

If those who would critique my life choices don't see in those choices the distinctive teachings and visible kingdom ways of Jesus—what he's for and against—they will never name me as his follower. They'll call me something else, and I don't want to be called anything else. I want people to ask, "What's the deal with him?"

Answer: "Him? Oh he's with Jesus."

———

Yes, something is wrong in the world. Sin has made a mess of people and place. There is a darkness over the land and in our hearts. But a more powerful brightness is present and proven in Jesus. My confidence is in him. In order to more fully know the privilege of being a co-conspirator with the Creator of the universe in the work of his kingdom, I'm submitting to my teacher, Jesus, resisting the temptation not to, and fleeing the shadows of the Dead Zone. This is the good to do. All ridiculous fools who follow Jesus can come near to God with clean hands, a pure heart, and a singularly focused mind. The grief over any time spent in the shadows can and should have its moment of mournful wail, high and scratchy. Then you get up and follow again. What else can you do when the words "Come, follow me" revisit and redirect? That's right, you follow the brightness.

We've already acknowledged that professing followers of Jesus disconnect from the controlling Story and live contrary to what they claim to believe. This is neither surprising nor a new revelation by any means. As God-directed reality becomes uncertain, so does identity. This is the argument for why one needs a potent worldview. A true worldview sees reality as God declares it. A worldview without a corresponding way of life is anemic and ineffective. Still a question remains: Regardless of its potency, how do we connect what we profess to believe about the world, or life, with the way we actually live in the world? How do we do it? Is it even possible?

I agree with my friend Steven Garber: Yes, it's entirely possible. Garber, in his book *The Fabric of Faithfulness,* talks about deciding which "facts, values, cares, and commitments" will give shape to life for a lifetime.[1] Gathered together as a worldview (or ways of being and knowing), these "facts, values, cares, and commitments" help followers reach the good goal of making and keeping the connection between belief and behavior. Be assured, the new way of Jesus can be sustained over a lifetime. God has not given his people an impossible task. Nevertheless, what Garber describes is not so much a how-to prescription as a description of the way the Spirit has worked in the lives of God's people throughout redemptive history.

In order to cooperate with God's agenda, to step into the Story, Garber encourages followers to develop what he calls "patterns of intentionality." These habits of heart and mind become our orientation; they frame the way we feel, think, imagine, speak, and do our creative work.

Garber has spent years studying followers of Jesus, listening to their stories. He's concluded that three things are always present in the life of every student-follower who steps into the Story with intentionality, who shuns consumer religion, and who faithfully lives out the new way to be human that Jesus inaugurated. In every case:

1. The student-follower is taught and believes the new way to be human, God's ways for the human family—ways sufficient to withstand the trials and challenges of life on earth. These ways become *convictions.* They belong to a tried-and-true formula: God's identity gives birth to reality. God's reality gives birth to human identity. Having their origin in God, these convictions stand tall against the false, incongruent, and insufficient ways and stories competing for human attention.

2. The student-follower meets a teacher who incarnates the new way, and the student sees that the new way to be human can be his or hers as well. This is an example of model *character* helping to develop new character in others. Embodiment shows the student that the new way is not beyond humanity, but is in fact made for humanity. It's a fit. When we see it, we know it. The new way has a magnetism because it has the *character DNA* of Jesus.

   The use of the word *teacher* should be seen in the broadest sense. We all instruct through word and work. Usually the student meets the teacher in the flesh, and a friendship develops. (I met my first teacher through the pages of a little booklet titled *Art and the Bible.* Though I never met my teacher in person, Francis Schaeffer was the first to really flesh out the new way for me. Now, many years later, it would be difficult to account for all the people I would credit as my teachers, known and unknown.)

3. The student-follower lives out the new way in *community* among like-minded and like-acting people. In community the student discovers the coherency of the new way of being and its application to the whole of life. In community, convictions and character are reinforced and named as norms for those who profess to follow. Community stewards memory. It is the *keeper* of the long memory of the Story *and* the *creator* of new memory congruent with the good story of those in history who walk with God and trust his Word. Together the community says: We hold to a story that we believe best explains reality. The community invites strangers, neighbors, and family to stand where they stand. "Have a look," the community says. Through word and work the community offers the best story regarding what's really most important to God, people, and

place. In community, people have not one teacher, but many. Not one brother or sister, but many. Not one friend, but many.[2]

Instead of having the past back with the East Tennessee Wilderness Prophet, what would it be like to have the present and a future? What would it be like to say to him, "Follow me as I follow Jesus—the certain Word?" What would it be like if he were to see me as his teacher? I wouldn't want him to follow as one disinterested or unengaged though. I'd want him to ask questions and express opinions. It wouldn't be right if he didn't test everything to see if it was good.

I'd begin with an invitation to experience community as we understand it in Beautiful View, Tennessee. I'd want him to come stand where we stand and have a look at our ways of being and doing—our patterns of intentionality. The best place to experience this in is our home in Tennessee—the Art House.

The Lily Life in Beautiful View, Tennessee

Today Andi and I consider our primary place of community our home, the Art House. This is where the facts, values, cares, and commitments that shape our lives are most evident. It's the place where we live intentionally and creatively, hoping to make the kingdom known and the new way visible.

The Art House has always been a place where God's people have worked out their stories. Built in 1912 in Bellevue, Tennessee, it was a country church for fifty-seven years. From the church's first event, a supper on the lawn at the dedication of the property in 1910, this location has been about God, people, and place. It's a nanocommunity reflecting the Creator's work, part of God's re-creation project. We rise each morning and do our best to cooperate.

We've owned the old Methodist church since late 1990, having purchased it from Lester and Sybil Moore. Owned is a truthful word, at least in terms of holding the deed, but cared for is a better, more accurate description. We've been tearing down, remodeling, building, shaping, and tending the old place for so long now that it's hard to remember a time when we weren't.

Recently, in order to line up yet another construction loan, the bank had the property appraised. Though it appraised for more than twice what we originally paid, the appraisal still fell short of what we've invested in the property over the years. I don't hold out hope for change in the future. We've had the house appraised several times over the years, in fact, and the response is always the same—there are no comparable properties in the Nashville area, and it's comparables that help establish value.

In the real-estate and loan business (as in most forms of commercial enterprise), similarity and sameness aid the appraisal of financial value. The presence of similarity in a system eliminates the need for personal knowledge, experienced and intuitive analysis, or imagination. It excludes the presence of faith, risk, and mystery. You don't have to bother asking if your piece of property is good, only if it's the same or similar to another. And if it is similar, what did the comparison properties appraise or sell for? Once you have your answer, you know the general value of your property.

Like so much appraisal of music, the real estate appraisal process has exasperated and depressed me. It's often caused me to wonder if I've been a good steward of the money and property God has entrusted me with. I understand that people who are serious about real estate don't spend more on a property than its worth. When they cash out, they're looking to make a profit. So far, by this standard, I haven't proved too serious. But I am. I have a different kind of seriousness, and it's a different kind of profit I'm looking for.

Our property has a value to us, to others, and to God that is greater than its commercial value. It stands as a marker for the cares and commitments that define our life on the planet. It is a place filled with story and meaning. Our mission is to live in such a way on the property that we contribute to its rich history. Our work is to leave behind a chapter that says loud and clear: "Here's the good that happened at a particular time in the history of God's people on earth, when two student-followers of Jesus were given stewardship over an old country church in Beautiful View, Tennessee." Following this line of thought, I love what Dorothy Day told her biographer Robert Coles: "Our lives are touched by those who lived centuries ago, and we hope that our lives will mean something to people who won't be alive until centuries from now. It's a great 'chain of being,' someone once told me, and I think our job is to do the best we can to hold up our small segment of the chain…to keep the chain connected, unbroken."[1]

That's what we're praying for and working to do—keep the chain unbroken.

In 1974, while we were still teenagers, Andi and I purchased a glossy book of stories and photos of unusual dwellings: geodesic domes, barns, structures made entirely out of scavenged pieces of junk, earth homes, an old mill, converted buses, and several converted churches. The book ignited our imaginations. Not only were many of the homes fantastic in the best sense of the word, but they represented the idea that a home could be not just a way station in a busy life but a work of art itself.

The book talked about houses as "an ongoing vision that went beyond four walls and a roof." According to the authors, "Some of the best shelters started life as something else: barns, schoolhouses, even churches." Every shelter pictured in the book "was once a dream."[2]

As I write I'm reading the book's introduction for the first time in twenty-nine years. Ironically, it closes with these words:

> If this book helps you to get your house out of your head and onto
> the ground…or even see through an old window differently, then
> it's a job well done. All it takes is getting started and enough
> friends to help you keep going. Later, it'll be a hassle for the tax
> assessor to figure the true value of your handiwork, but the first
> time you sit down and look around at it, you'll know![3]

The story of our home began in 1910, when John and Anna Thompson donated land on the north side of the Big Harpeth River on Old

Harding for the construction of a new Methodist church. A building committee composed of T. L. Herrin Jr., J. F. Thompson and Will Horn were appointed to supervise the work. In June of 1910, the homecoming with dinner on the ground was held to celebrate the donation of the land and the hope of construction. All went well, and the Bellevue Methodist Church was formally dedicated September 20, 1912.

After fifty-plus years the people outgrew their little country church, and in March of 1969 construction began on a larger, more modern building just down the road at Harpeth Parkway West. When the congregation moved into its new home in September of 1969, the old building became the Methodist Church Annex.

Mr. and Mrs. Charles Dunlap bought the building in 1974. They were the first to use it as a residence, and that's about all anyone knows. The next occupant was the son of Lester and Sybil Moore. The Moores purchased the church for him as a remodeling project and home for his family. After the son lost interest and moved out of state, the Moores took over.

"My sisters and friends thought I was crazy," remembers Sybil. "I had just fallen in love with that old church. It was so peaceful. We moved in without even a bed to sleep on and worked every day to fulfill our plans to make the old church our home."

And a home they made—a beautiful one filled with books and antiques and overall uniqueness. They enjoyed their home but were also pleased to share it. People used the big room for weddings, receptions, and parties. Through the Bed and Breakfast Host Homes of Tennessee, they rented rooms to travelers for fifty-five dollars a day, including breakfast.

For long-time residents of Bellevue, the church is a local fixture. *This is where I was baptized. This is where I shared my first kiss.* Old newspaper clippings record some of its history. For instance, one year the Bellevue-Harpeth Historical Society sponsored an "Old-Fashioned Box Supper and Sociable" at the old church, where state senator Douglas Henry Jr. acted

as master of ceremonies for the cakewalk, folk singers Jim and Louise
Hardaway shared songs from the Revolutionary and Civil War periods,
and Pastor Herb McCoy of the Bellevue Christian Church performed his
card tricks.

I love knowing this history. It helps me visualize our place in the
ongoing Story that God is telling. It reminds me that we have stepped
into a much larger Story than just our own.

And here is how we came to this place: In 1989 we moved from Sacramento to Nashville, to the community of Bellevue, twenty minutes south-
west of the city. According to the plan we'd made back in California, we set
out to buy a house in a subdivision off Old Harding Road. You can't get
too far in Bellevue without using Old Harding. It's one of the main arter-
ies, and the old white church sits alongside it, up a bit, slightly elevated.

In August of 1990 I'd toured Europe. I always have lots of time for
thinking and writing while traveling, and this trip was no exception. I
wrote in my journal:

> There is a generation of Christian artists in our midst who are
> more used to following formulas than following the Creator. They
> ask questions like, "What do I have to do to be a success in CCM
> [contemporary Christian music]?" They are button pushers only
> interested in knowing what buttons to push in order to achieve
> their desired results. Artists like this may flourish and be top sell-
> ers, but as a model for creating art in the context of the Christian
> faith, they are bankrupt to contribute. They are not bad people or
> necessarily bad artists; they are merely sheep without a shepherd.

Strong words for sure. I was confused and troubled by the kind of
ambition I was seeing in young artists moving to Nashville, the growing

hub of Christian music. I was becoming increasingly convinced that God wanted me to do some particular work in addition to my music. But the work was still a vapor. I'd talk about it but make no sense to anyone but myself.

The Spirit-words of Ezekiel gave some clarity: "You have not strengthened the weak or healed the sick or bound up the injured. You have not brought back the strays or searched for the lost. You have ruled them harshly and brutally. So they were scattered because there was no shepherd, and when they were scattered they became food for all the wild animals. My sheep wandered over all the mountains and on every high hill. They were scattered over the whole earth, and no one searched or looked for them" (34:4-6).

This passage and the words of Jesus to Peter in the book of John rang like timpani rolls in my skull. God was saying to me, "If you love me, feed my sheep. Go get them, care for them and feed them. Give them a place of shelter." That's how I began to dream of a place where young artists could gather for friendship, community, and teaching. I gave my imaginary place a name: the Art House.

One day in the fall of 1990, a for-sale sign went up in the yard of the old white church. Andi, the kids, and I passed it in the car, and I commented: "Maybe that's the Art House." As a lark, we took some friends and solicited a look inside. We made it clear we were more curious than interested. This was fine with the Moores. They put us at ease, gave us a great tour of the home, and we visited for a good two hours or more. The place had the power to inspire, and it was hard to push down the thought of owning it. That would be impossible though. We could barely afford our new house and the recording studio we'd just begun building.

After the look-see with our friends, Andi and I returned for another visit. Yep, still great. Still full of promise. What were we doing though? We walked to our car, sat in silence, and cried like babies. "Why are you crying?" "I don't know. Why are *you* crying?" We drove a mile down the road to our one-year-old house and asked, "God, why are we crying?"

We talked, we prayed. I couldn't sleep for grinding my teeth. We talked and prayed some more. We argued more than a little. Lester told me he'd carry the mortgage note if I could come up with a down payment, which may as well have been a million dollars. We simply could not afford it. Besides that, if we could have, it would mean maintaining three properties—home, studio, and the Art House. All of it was beyond us.

At this same time Sparrow Records approached me about leasing some of my older recordings. I drove down to Music Row, to the first Sparrow Records office in Nashville, and met with Billy Ray Hearn. We discussed the financial part of the deal. He offered me one amount, and I countered him with a figure that matched Lester's down payment. "All right," Billy Ray said, "we'll do it for that."

At the mortgage closing, Sybil Moore cried big tears of regret, and my caring wife comforted her. With no malice intended, it's probable that we signed one of the craziest and most convoluted mortgages in history that day, but we walked out with the keys to the Art House.

God knew we couldn't do it alone, so he sent some very special people to help with the work. Our pastor, Scotty Smith, eagerly affirmed our intentions and signed up for the ride. Scotty would be the Art House anchor, teaching a weekly Bible Study attended by anywhere from 100 to 150 people, mostly twenty-somethings. For many, this would be their first serious study of the biblical Story.

Barbara Haynes was a board member and a great help to us. Billy Ray Hearn gifted us so that we could put central heating and air in the building. Our first Art House worker was Nick Barré, a young youth pastor from Florida via Oral Roberts University. Nick and his best friend, Doug McKelvey, moved to Nashville to be a part of the Art House. Their help was invaluable, as was a Wheaton College intern named Jay Swartzendruber.

Subsequent Art House workers were the author-educator David Dark, and Russ Ramsey, now a pastor in Kansas City. Many gracious people, too many to mention here, volunteered their talents and resources in service of the work.

According to our first brochure in the beginning, "The Art House Foundation was birthed in order to benefit Christians called to create art within the context of their faith."

It was "our dream that God would use the Art House Foundation to prepare artists filled with the Spirit of God, with skill, ability, and knowledge (Exodus 35:31). That these artists, having been well equipped, would venture into both the church and the world to create powerful and astonishing works of creativity. And that these works, created with passion and honesty, would serve the church and the culture as God in his wisdom would ordain."

A little later on, the Art House expanded its purpose "to encourage Christians, both artists and nonartists alike, to develop their minds—to think 'Christianly' about all of life, to live artfully, and to apply the truth to their lives and their art."

Either way, the Art House was always more than a concept. It was about place—the old country church we'd fallen in love with: "A place where we can be reminded through fellowship, study, and prayer what it means to create art to the glory of God—where we can exchange ideas, search the Scriptures together, and listen to gifted speakers reveal something about their own journey through the arts and the Christian faith."

Today the Art House is clearly a home, but it's like a small campus as well. In 1992 we built a recording studio and offices on the property, and in 1993 we moved into the church building. Since that time we've been working to create a place that reflects God's excellence. Andi has developed large cottage and shade gardens, lining the property with horticultural surprises. Spring is like the Fourth of July, with one plant after another sending out fireworks. Though now only Andi and I live on the property, people come to the Art House every day for all kinds of reasons that transcend the normal workings of a family home. I once thanked an artist for attending a study on following Jesus. "Are you kidding?" he said. "I'm always eager to visit here—I know something good is going to happen."

I can't help but think this is what motivates people to come here. Musicians, engineers, and producers work in the studio. People drop by for business and spiritual counsel—or tips from Andi, the Master Gardener. Others come for a meal or to stay for a week. Motivations and needs for visiting are always different. We pray and ask God to bring us the people he wants us to love, do good to, and prepare for works of service. It's intuitive, liquid, and spontaneous. There's no registration, and no one gets evaluated by an admission committee. People find out by word of mouth that the Art House is a pastoral ministry of caring for people through teaching, the arts, and hospitality. We've always assumed that those who are meant to come will come.

We're more intentional and less spontaneous when it comes to Art House events. These are times set apart to listen to speakers, to give ear to musical artists, or to study under a particular teacher for an evening, a weekend, or several weeks. It's of no little significance that the Art House sits next to the Harpeth River. The Harpeth is a small but important feeder river in the greater Nashville area. All of its incarnations feed into the Cumberland, a river than runs downtown through the heart of business and culture in Nashville. The Cumberland eventually feeds into the vast Tennessee River and its system of lakes and reservoirs. Next, rivers like the Big Sandy and Hatchie shoot west off the Tennessee waterway and work their way to the mighty Mississippi, then down to the Mississippi Sound. Finally, the waters travel to the Gulf of Mexico, where they take their place among the oceans of the world, and thus touch the shores of the major cities of the world as well. This describes the flow of our out-bound work of story and music.

~~~

More than fifty years ago Frank Capra made a delightfully odd movie titled *You Can't Take It with You.* In the film we meet Mr. Poppins, a frus-trated inventor who toils behind an adding machine all day in the Depres-sion era. One day he meets the good-hearted, eccentric Grandpa Martin Vanderhof, patriarch of the loopy, free-spirited Sycamore family. After some prompting, Poppins shows Grandpa a toy he has made. Delighted with Mr. Poppins's skill, Grandpa asks, "How'd you like to come over to our house and work on your gadgets?"

"Really?" says Mr. Poppins. "That would be wonderful. But how would I live?"

"Same way we do," says Grandpa.

"Same way? Well, who takes care of you?"

"The same one that takes care of the lilies of the field, Mr. Poppins. If you want to, come on over and become a lily too."

Mr. Poppins looks up with a smile. "Me, a lily of the field?"

The way of the lily is the Art House way. We love God and do as we please. Our pleasure is to please God and to love what he loves both locally and globally. Most recently the focus of our outbound love has been Africa's victims of AIDS and famine.

In December 2002, U2's Bono dropped by the Art House to talk about the African AIDS emergency. He founded an organization called DATA, a dual acronym that stands for Debt, AIDS, Trade in Africa *in return for* Democracy, Accountability, Transparency in Africa. The Art House and Awake work closely with DATA.[4] Several musical artists in our Nashville community gathered to hear Bono tell the story of Africa's AIDS emergency. Many left that day motivated to give time and resources, awaken their audiences to the emergency, call the White House, and put DATA information in their CD booklets.[5]

Caring for God's creativity, whether that means music or people in need on the other side of the world, is what shapes our home life and ad hoc Art House community. We promote storytelling and storied living, not through well-executed, easily defined programs, but by creating the environment and potential for good to occur. Our work of hospitality, art, and study is about this one thing. It all stems from the belief that home can and should be an instrument of grace, an engine of truth and beauty. Home should be a place where the best thoughts on what's really important are sought out and communicated, where imagination and creativity are encouraged to take shape for the good of Jesus followers, and the world that watches and listens.

The Art House is a sacramental place. It holds memory and reminds us of who we are and what artful, spiritual student-followers of Jesus are called to be and do. We stumble after this good goal with compass in hand and heart, grateful for meaningful work and the rich, diverse community the Art House holds and attracts.

This is why, if I could, I would invite the East Tennessee Wilderness Prophet over to the house. He could hear our word and see our work—our storytelling and storied living.

The New Way of
Relationships

Easter Quigley's Slippery Pearls

When I write a novel, it will be about men and women. That's where the drama lives, as any man or woman will tell you. The woman in my novel will be named Easter Quigley, a name I lifted off a grave marker at the Sutter Cemetery, in Sutter, California. Imagine with me…

Easter Quigley had hips with dramatic divots, red hair more blonde than crimson, a better than average overall symmetry to her body, and on a good day, the smile of a watermelon just sliced in two.

It was not a good day.

"The women are the strong ones," she blubbered through clinched teeth, stepping across the gutter into the street. Easter was not herself. She'd exercised after work, waived the routine shower, stripped down to her sports bra and panties, and pulled over her head and down her sticky skin something Grandma called a shift. The dress, a flowery print, was cheap and without shape. It joined with Easter's frame to incarnate a cottage garden smelling of neglected underarms. It wasn't her habit to choose this way.

Easter's haste was due to an unoriginal idea that had come to her less than five minutes before: She would get in her car and drive right over to Michael's apartment. Yes, that's what she'd do; she would take her stinky, flowery self four blocks over and confront him. If he did not come clean with the truth (or if he *did come clean* with the truth), she would kill him—slowly.

Her friend Greta had told her, "It's hit or miss, Easter. You never know what you're going to get, a hero or a villain."

Easter had refused to cave to pessimism. Still, she thought, there must be some way of knowing, of avoiding doing the hokey-pokey with one villain after another, putting your whole self in, and then suddenly having to pull your whole self out.

Easter beeped the Jetta and climbed in. She gripped the steering wheel until her knuckles whitened. *Is it the sex or the lying that is most offensive?* she wondered.

The Jetta moved away from the curb. As it did, the left rear tire chewed into a mosaic of broken glass carelessly left in the gutter. Much-delayed tears escaped her eyes.

Four blocks later, there was no sign of his car. It might be in the back. No. He's so unfaithful he can't even be trusted to be present for the obligatory postextracurricular copulation confrontation. *Hate,* she thought, *takes a lot of effort.*

After a week of unrelenting teary phone messages from Michael, hair the consistency of olive oil, sweat pants, and *Oprah,* she came to terms with the "whole sorry mess" and decided she was "so much better off without him." Just by considering the currency of one week's absence, Easter came to see great wealth in never having to tolerate Michael's annoying habits again. It was unnatural to decide on a Monday to fly someplace like Bali or Vietnam on a Friday, purchase a bicycle on arrival and pedal off on a tour of the countryside for a week. Once back on U.S. soil, he would work some detail or anecdote of his adventures into every conversation, regardless of its relevance. And the man was chronically chef-dependent, too, eating out nearly every night. For some reason this filled Easter with disgust.

As a sign and seal of their breakup, she sent Michael a box, via FedEx, of personal items he'd left at her apartment. "I made the villainous one sign for his own toothbrush," she gloated, "it was a most satisfying expenditure."

When the time was almost right, Easter called her mother.

Andi and I have been together since we were fourteen and fifteen—married at eighteen and nineteen. As of this writing we've been married for twenty-eight years. These facts alone put us in a small minority. The average age of marriage for men is twenty-eight, women twenty-five. The average length of a marriage is a little over seven years. If you count the years we dated before marriage, we've been together for thirty-two years. Of those thirty-two years, ten were spent as wanderers living in the world where the Easter Quigleys dwell. Over and over we put our whole selves in only to jerk them out again. Back then we were still in the Dead Zone and had yet to follow Jesus in the new way. At just the right time though, we were pulled from the wreckage, and by the light of God we stumbled after Jesus.

It's from this beginning, history, and vantage point that we watch men and women circle around each other in love and marriage. From where we stand, we observe single men and women in their loneliness and desire. And we listen to the ache of relationship, marriage, and sex gone wrong. The Art House has given us front-row seats for this type of theater—a kind of teaching hospital. We watch, listen, learn, and wonder. Mostly wonder.

What I wonder is whether people have any idea of the consequences of sin. I wonder if they are in on the secret of what God is doing with man and woman in marriage in the world. You want the truth? Of course you do. We don't live like the Fall is real, like sin is real. We think that if we're careful and clever enough, we'll make a great choice in a mate and avoid a lot of pain and suffering. I'm not suggesting that people shouldn't make good choices or pick compatible mates. What I've observed is that people often avoid marriage for fear that a potential lover may have too many problems or issues. I want to cry out with the language of Dr. Seuss, "Oh, the problems and issues you will have!"

Followers of Jesus are tempted to think that the Easter Quigleys of the world are the saddest victims of misspent love. It's true that giving your body away to an untrustworthy human is the way of sin and pain. No question. But *every* relationship is touched by sin and pain, even those founded on *True Love Waits* and *I Kissed Dating Goodbye.*

No serious student-follower committed to loving the opposite sex in marriage or singleness can avoid the fact that sin has made a wreck of the way to be human. Now, after the pattern of the King of Twists, every good way has a twist in it. The consequence of sin has dramatically affected the Creational and Relational Norms of human integrity.

First, as we looked at earlier, the Creational Norm is twisted up. God's creative Word (earth and sky) is no longer the embodiment of care and provision it once was. Living on earth and caring for it is frustrating work. Caring for any creativity has its frustrations.

The Relational Norm is twisted up as well, and the intimate friendship of God, man, and woman is fractured and frustrated. God's will and his way (his spoken Word) are no longer the controlling Story of man and woman. Self-interest, self-importance, fear, and distrust have replaced the God-human conversation regarding matters of mutual interest and importance.

Serious followers of the new way acknowledge and accept that everything is twisted up. They figure this into their thinking about relationships. I've met some hysterical optimists and some genuine lovers who take exception to this view. It's too pessimistic. I think it's realistic. I know that lovers believe their union will be the exception, but to a couple, all will be proved wrong. My boldness is not my own. It comes from the Story:

Man is given to following the creational track, moving in the opposite direction of God and integrity. Man says: "I will dominate my creation." He moves from dominion to domination, from stewardship to ownership, and from covenant relationship to self-rule. Instead of man and woman with God in God's place under God's rule, the way for man has become: *Man, separate from God, in his own place under his own rule.*

Woman is given to following the relational track, moving in the opposite direction of God and integrity. Woman says: "I will desire my relationship(s) over everything else." She moves from dominion to domination of relational desire, from stewardship to relinquishment, acquiescence, or control (that is, passive and active forms of twistedness). She moves from the covenant relationship of God, people, and place to self-rule or living under man's rule. Most often in history, the way for woman is: *Woman in man's place under man's rule.*

These are general distinctions. Nevertheless, with various exceptions allowed for, these two gender tracks provide a historically accurate illustration of the post-Fall ways of man and woman.

In the Story, God told man and woman the consequences of their sin and how the direction of their lives would change from that point forward. To the woman God said, "I will greatly increase your pains in childbearing; with pain you will give birth to children. Your desire will be for your husband, and he will rule over you" (Genesis 3:16).

The dominion/caretaking role included reproduction. Had sin not entered the world, this would have been a wholly and mutually satisfying vocation—from the pleasure of sexual intimacy to the pleasure of mutually creating and bringing into God's world a new creation. Nevertheless, the woman (and not the man) would still bear the primary responsibility for carrying the child in her womb.

I have some thoughts on the issue of the woman's pain increasing. I see the pain as *total in scope.* It is physical, emotional, intellectual, and spiritual. Women know the physical pain is intense, but it may be that the lasting pain is primarily relational. The pain of bringing a child into the world may in fact last a lifetime (as many parents will attest). I also think that some part of the idea of pain is connected to frustration, disappointment, and dissatisfaction. It is the pain of unrealized expectations having to do with this one remarkable aspect of human creativity.

A mutual, one-flesh act may bring a child into the world, but history shows that it's the half-flesh of woman that nurtures and grows the child. What should be a wholly and mutually satisfying vocation isn't allowed to be. It's frustrated by absence when only presence will do. Where's man? He's busy dominating the creation under self-rule. Mary Stewart Van Leeuwen taps into part of this when she writes, "The woman is being warned [in Genesis] that she will experience an unreciprocated longing for intimacy with the man."[1] Unfortunately for the woman, neither the critical role of childbearing nor intimacy with man will provide the kind of satisfaction and completion she longs for. At its most basic, the consequence of sin for the woman is this: She will have an unsatisfied hunger and thirst that no human relationship can fill.

Exceptions acknowledged, directionally speaking, sin moved the woman from her authoritative role in dominion to a new distorted desire. From this point in the Story forward, she will desire mutual relationship (with both sexes) far more than her codominion role. Woman will have a long memory for the norm of one flesh and relational intimacy. In general, this memory and desire will be greater than the desire to fulfill the stewardship calling to care for everything—the relational and the creational. It's in the balance of creation stewardship that the man will suffer his own painful consequences.

To man God said,

Because you listened to your wife and ate from the tree about which I commanded you, "You must not eat of it,"

Cursed is the ground because of you;
>   through painful toil you will eat of it
>   all the days of your life.
It will produce thorns and thistles for you,
>   and you will eat the plants of the field.
By the sweat of your brow
>   you will eat your food
until you return to the ground,
>   since from it you were taken;
for dust you are
>   and to dust you will return. (Genesis 3:17-19)

There has been a tendency to read "Because you listened to your wife" through a contemporary lens of gender and faith issues. We can't afford to do that. We must read it in the context of the Story. We know that the man was present at the conversation. His human presence assumes human hearing and listening. The implication isn't, "You shouldn't have listened to your wife. Don't take orders from her!" It is *you listened to your wife,* to what she said, to the way she answered the questions and statements posed to her by the serpent. Hold on to this idea.

Before we can go further we have to return to an earlier part of the Story. We do this to keep ourselves on track. How important is the Word of God in the first two chapters of Genesis? It is a creative Word of will from the very beginning, isn't it? From "let us make" (Genesis 1:26) to "you must not" (Genesis 2:17). Always and everywhere the Word of God is creating the stuff of story and providing the controlling narrative. A representative of God, especially the first representative (the man), carefully handles all of God's Word, whether it be his creativity, will, rule, or truth about the way things are supposed to be. From the beginning man is to be this kind of worker. *The work is to care for God's revealed Word in creation and his revealed Word in what has been spoken.* Stewardship applies to both, and both are intertwined. Even fast-forwarding to the New Testament you see this. It's likely that Paul remembered back to man's failure when he encouraged Timothy: "Do your best to present yourself to God as one approved, a workman who does not need to be ashamed and who correctly handles the word of truth" (2 Timothy 2:15).

Now we can return to the source text again: "Because you listened to your wife and ate from the tree about which I commanded you, 'You must not eat of it,' Cursed is the ground because of you; through painful toil you will eat of it all the days of your life" (Genesis 3:17).

The man's sin is not that he simply listened to his wife, but that he listened, said nothing, and did the very thing he was commanded not to do. His silence is deafening, and it's by his silence that man separates what God has joined together. He doesn't testify of the knowledge given him; instead he's timid. He doesn't guard the truth; he doesn't steward God's relational and creational Word. He was first to see the garden, first to see the trees, first to hear the commandment, first to know the Story, and first to step into the Story. Though not the first to violate the commandment in eating of the tree, he *is* the first human responsible to God for creation (which included the woman). He failed to care for all that was entrusted to him. His stewardship failure set the stage for the failures of his son Cain. "Am I my brother's keeper?" Cain asked (Genesis 4:9).

This is speculation, but it's plausible that the couple's unity had already begun to be a substitute for the organizing Story of God and people living under God's rule (heart-sin before behavior). This humanistic impulse becomes even clearer later in Babel. In Eden it's possible that the man's allegiance to himself and the woman had begun to redefine reality. Was man's glory (the woman and her excellence) overtaking the glory of God in the mind of man? Perhaps he had already begun to trade the truth of God for a lie by worshiping the creation (the woman) rather than the Creator. Again, this is pure speculation.

Different from the woman's consequence, man moves from domin-ion to sinful male domination. He abuses the power and authority origi-nally given to both man and woman. Now man dominates even the bone of his bones and the flesh of his flesh. He actively and passively dominates everything to scratch fruit from the earth, to meet personal agendas of achievement, to make a name for himself, and to create wealth. Eventu-ally, man will even try to use domination to bring the kingdom to pass. He selfishly dominates at the expense of the oneness and unity of purpose he is called to with God and woman. No matter how clever man is, how hard he works or doesn't work, or how much pleasure or wealth he accu-mulates, he is never satisfied. Perfection and satisfaction slip through his fingers like slippery pearls. As with woman, man continues to hunger and thirst. This is the direction that sin took man and woman.

God allowed sin its consequences, knowing that it would *ensure humankind's dissatisfaction.* Ultimate unity, intimacy, and purpose exist only with the Creator. Only God can save man and woman. Only God can fill their need, quench their thirst. Only God can deliver them from evil and the consequences of sin.

I've been writing about the first man and woman, Adam and Eve. But you know that I'm writing about you, about me, about every human being since the beginning. Something's wrong, and it's not right—and it's okay to talk about it and name it. There is a darkness over the land and in the hearts of people everywhere. Sin is real. Men and women stand in the shad-ows of the Dead Zone by the grace of God, or they remain in it awaiting rescue. We shouldn't lie about the human condition, fake it, or forget it. We can't pretend that nothing's wrong when something clearly is.

Recovering the Strategic Team

The way of God—the way that Jesus renews—is for the differentiated sexes of male and female to hold the Relational and Creational Norms together as a whole. This is what is meant by integrity. The relational and creational are not meant to be separated or taken over and distorted by one particular sex. The generalization that men are in charge of dominion and women are in charge of relationships should not hold true. When sin separated what God had joined together, the way of being human and the unity of mission were separated. *The integrated couple became two disintegrated individuals.* Individualism is as old as sin.

I'm of the opinion that the story of the first man and woman is quite clear: Man is not the sole caretaker of God's interests on earth, with woman trailing behind as some sort of obsequious helper. Her first order of help as a creature was to be the only right completion of humanity. The first help she gave correlates with the need God announced: "It is not good for the man to be alone" (Genesis 2:18). This is the same need man recognized as he cataloged the animal world: the absence of a corresponding, complementary, sexually differentiated living being. Because the woman was this help first, out of her identity and image-bearing goodness she could then be a help in other ways. Likewise, the man could be a help to her in carrying out the mandate given to both of them.

They were a *strategic team* assembled by God, for each other, to reveal God's excellence. The Story teaches that both man and woman were called to fill and subdue, to be fruitful and multiply, to exercise dominion and manage creation. It is possible to hold this in place as you come to other texts in the Story, and to do so while maintaining that male and female are created and equipped with unique and complementary abilities and assignments—yet not identical ones. It is especially essential to hold all of this together in light of the marriage leadership role given to men. This role becomes unbelievable and abused unless these and other equally important facts support it.

The new way of Jesus brings more clarity. In Ephesians 5 Paul taught the gathering of followers, "Be imitators of God, therefore, as dearly loved children and live a life of love, just as Christ loved us and gave himself up for us as a fragrant offering and sacrifice to God" (verses 1-2). He was gently teaching them: "Listen to God's Word, watch God work. What do you see and hear? Do these in a way that is distinctly human after the pattern of the King of the kingdom, Jesus."

The principle is this: Those who know they are loved want to imitate those who love them. In practice, love should undergird and define this new way of living. How do we love? In imitation of Messiah Jesus. We give ourselves away to God, one another, and to the care of all that God loves. We set aside our agendas to live out God's agenda of redemption and renewal in the kingdom way. In view of God's mercy, how can we not? This is our spiritual act of worship, a good and pleasing sacrifice.

Further into Ephesians 5, the follower Paul got more specific: "Submit to one another out of reverence for Christ" (verse 21).

This is often used in the gender debate to buttress various arguments. Is this even necessary? If you let the verse stand in its context, it is a commandment to all followers to submit to one another. It's inclusive of every possible relationship in the gathering of Jesus people, husband and wife included. As Galatians 3:28 says, "There is neither Jew nor Greek, slave nor free, male nor female, for you are all one in Christ Jesus." This and the first two verses of Ephesians 5 yield a strong foundation for following in the sacrificial, other-centered way of Jesus.

Paul offered more though, adding specifics to his basic message about imitation and submission. He began filling in the details as to what love looks like within covenant marriage. He told the wives to "submit to your husbands as to the Lord. For the husband is the head of the wife as Christ is the head of the church, his body, of which he is the Savior. Now as the church submits to Christ, so also wives should submit to their husbands in everything" (verses 22-24).

Next Paul addressed the husbands:

> Husbands, love your wives, just as Christ loved the church and gave himself up for her to make her holy, cleansing her by the washing with water through the word, and to present her to himself as a radiant church, without stain or wrinkle or any other blemish, but holy and blameless. In this same way, husbands ought to love their wives as their own bodies. He who loves his wife loves himself. After all, no one ever hated his own body, but he feeds and cares for it, just as Christ does the church—for we are members of his body. (verses 25-30)

Then Paul switched back to talking in general terms about the church, but watch how he did it: " 'For this reason a man will leave his father and mother and be united to his wife, and the two will become one flesh.' This is a profound mystery—but I am talking about Christ and the church. However, each one of you also must love his wife as he loves himself, and the wife must respect her husband" (verses 31-33).

The fact that these verses and others from 1 Timothy have caused women, in particular, so much pain is a sad commentary on our failure to be the people of God. The whole assembly of followers has suffered as well, and God and his Word have been maligned. I wish we could start fresh with new words for obedience and submission. Our only hope is to see them anew in the new way of Jesus. This is, I believe, a well-placed hope.

Let's bounce back to the end of Ephesians 4 for further context about being imitators of God. Ephesians 4:31-32 says, "Get rid of all bitterness, rage and anger, brawling and slander, along with every form of malice. Be kind and compassionate to one another, forgiving each other, just as in Christ God forgave you."

Now we can read Ephesians 5:1-2 again: "Be imitators of God, therefore, as dearly loved children and live a life of love, just as Christ loved us and gave himself up for us as a fragrant offering and sacrifice to God."

The new way is to rid yourself of the old relational ways and step into the Relational Norm of Messiah: kindness, compassion, and forgiveness. Imitate God in this way and love as Jesus loved you. Obediently submit your whole being as a sacrifice to God and his ways of being human found in his Son. Even more specifically, connect this to the centrality of the cross of Jesus in the Story. In Matthew 16:24, Jesus said to his disciples, "If anyone would come after me, he must deny himself and take up his cross and follow me." These words, and those like them recorded in the other Gospels, are at the heart of following in the new way to be human. Jesus is making it clear that anyone who professes to be his student-follower must experience self-denial and martyrdom (in whatever shape it takes). He says in Mark 8:35, "For whoever wants to save his life will lose it, but whoever loses his life for me and for the gospel will save it." And in Luke 14:33: "In the same way, any of you who does not give up everything he has cannot be my disciple."

These are difficult words for men and women. Each word and phrase is God's hand drawing a line in the heart. *Will my direct representatives listen to my relational Word, or follow in the way of Adam and Eve?* It is natural for people to say it can't be this way. But it is spiritual to see that it must. This is why Paul wrote in 1 Corinthians 1:18: "For the message of the cross is foolishness to those who are perishing, but to us who are being saved it is the power of God."

Now I'll speak strongly. Men and women, please don't even think about what "submit to your husbands as to the Lord" means until you've taken to heart what we've just studied. The Jesus way is the way of obedient submission to the will of the Father. Paul was saying to women: "With respect to your husbands, imitate Jesus in this way." When Paul said the husband is the head of the wife as Christ is the head of the church, he was telling the Ephesians a controlling story that has two tiers.

The first tier: In the Creation Story, man is created first. He was given meaningful work in the garden where he clearly understood his authoritative, caretaking role. With authority and understanding, he cataloged and named God's creativity in great detail. All of this occurred before the woman was created. While doing his work the man came to realize that he had no complement, no differentiated sex like the animals he'd been working with. So God created woman as the only suitable help for man's need. But the way God created woman was completely unique to creation. In the very beginning the sole power of his creational Word spoke everything into existence (including the dust of man). For woman, God employed a new method or innovation. He enlisted the man, his head living being, in the creative process. Man's co-creating role was strange though.

God caused the man to fall into a deep sleep. The Story doesn't tell us if the man knew he was about to sacrifice a rib for God's new creative project. While the man was sleeping, God surgically removed one of the man's ribs. We know this because God closed up the wound with flesh. From this one rib, God made woman. By the wound and sacrifice of the head living being, in the creative power of God, woman came into being. She was like man, yet different. She had her own excellence, which in turn spoke of both man's and God's.

From here we should stop for a moment and mentally reconnect with everything we've studied so far in terms of the couple's mutual cultural mission and mutual dignity. The challenge is to hold on to all of it and not drop any.

According to the Story, man is clearly the head living being and leader from the beginning. But it does little good to acknowledge this unless we also recognize that man's first act for woman is an act of sacrifice and obedience to the ways of God. His is also an act that began before the woman was brought into being. This is a preview of the Excellent Man to come, Jesus. *From Genesis forward, there is no story of headship or authority that does not come without a mission requiring obedient sacrifice.* Throughout the Story, obedient sacrificial work gives birth to new creation.

To acknowledge in word and work that the husband is the head of the wife as Christ is the head of the church is to honor God's Creational and Relational Norms for reality. It is about the integrity of God's first image bearer, not about man's superiority (of which he has none with respect to woman). Where authentic authority exists, it is given by God for his good will. If authority is not sacrificial service to God, people, and place, it is something other than what God intended. It is ill will and reproduces itself in hearts as more of the same. Authority that does not serve itself but lives and dies to serve others is the only authority among humans in the new way.

By writing that the husband is to be the head of the wife as Messiah is the head of all the followers, Paul was subverting all male gender stereotypes, ancient and modern. The kind of husbandlike authority Jesus modeled is the only authority men should have and women should respect. In Matthew 28:18, Jesus said that all authority in heaven and on earth had been given to him. Speaking about his own life, Jesus said in John 10:18, "No one takes it [my life] from me, but I lay it down of my own accord. I have authority to lay it down and authority to take it up again. This command I received from my Father."

Understanding the Jesus way is essential to understanding what is being asked of women and men. Even as the Authoritative Man, Jesus will lay down his life or take it up again based on the relational will of his Father. The woman is given magisterial authority in the Creation Story, and this authoritative role holds throughout time. It is not identical to the authority given to the man, but neither is it any less important.

This teaching on authority, which so many have found to be difficult, is not a new Pauline teaching. Women are being instructed to follow in the Jesus way, to yield to authority while holding on to the good authority and role given them in the beginning. Put another way: *Follow in the way of the cross and lay down your life while holding on to what I assigned you from the beginning. Do not assert your human glory or insist on your rights.* God wants women to know when they live by his ways, fighting for rights should not be necessary.

Now continue to hold on to all of this and don't drop any of it. God is calling women to remember their role in creative history. Don't leave man alone. In or out of marriage, partner with man in the care of all of God's creativity (and in marriage, especially the care of each other). Most important, don't even think about having a relational life (with men) without first having a relational life with the Creator. This is and always has been God's invitation to life—and never a violation of human rights. Women are made to want it all: relationship and creation stewardship. This is the norm. Because women are differentiated from men, their fulfillment of the Relational and Creational Norms will naturally be different. Nevertheless, the calling remains: Cogovern with men and fulfill both norms faithfully.

The second tier of this controlling Story has to do with Jesus as the husband of the bride, the church. It's no accident that Paul quoted Genesis 2:24 in Ephesians 5: " 'For this reason a man will leave his father and mother and be united to his wife, and the two will become one flesh.' This is a profound mystery—but I am talking about Christ and the church" (verses 31-32).

For the purpose of re-creation, Jesus left his home to look for his bride, unite with her, show her unprecedented sacrificial love, and encourage her to work alongside him in a life-changing and eternal work. This is the model role of every husband-follower of Jesus. It's this authoritative role that woman is being asked to yield to, nothing more and nothing less.

Whereas the wound of Adam helped woman come into being, the wounds of Jesus heal her of sin and re-create her in the new way of rightness (1 Peter 2:24). Unlike the wound that helped to create woman, the wounds of Jesus were not patched with flesh from the Creator. Blood flowed from his wounds to secure atonement for his people so that their re-creation could begin. He acted on behalf of generations of people who had yet to come into being.

Jesus, the head (and bridegroom), joins with the body (and bride) to become one flesh. He is clearly "the head of the body, the church; he is the beginning and the firstborn from among the dead, so that in everything he might have the supremacy" (Colossians 1:18). Women should never worry about man's having supremacy. It's not his to have. All student-followers are one in Jesus, members of one body, his body. Man's authority may be related to being the firstborn among living beings on earth, but Jesus shows himself to be the better man. He comes living, dying, and living. Unlike man, whose authority is to live, Jesus has authority over life and death. His resurrection power is delivering all of creation from sin and death. He is Love Supreme in everything.

<hr />

Paul wanted husbands to be intentional followers of the Love Supreme, to lay down their lives for their wives. He called men to cooperate with God in the re-creation of their relational and creational integrity and to use this integrity in the care of their wives. They are to live the Word and work of Jesus, to make imaginative and creative choices that encourage and enable their wives to be storytellers with good storied living. Each day on earth, as God's direct representative, the husband has the opportunity to present woman to God as God's artwork in process. With enthusiasm, man should say to God, "Look, Father, at how I'm caring for this woman you've entrusted to me. Look at how she's returning stepwise to the good role in creative history you gave her. She is following your Son, Jesus, and as a result is holy and blameless before you. She is radiant and beautiful. You are her supreme authority, and she lives for your agenda here on earth. She is my coworker in spreading the good news of the kingdom and caring for all your creativity. I submit to her out of respect and reverence for your excellence in creating her beauty and intelligence. I submit to her out of respect for the creative authority you gave her in the beginning. I see her and her word and work, and I know you are worthy of all honor, praise, and glory!"

Likewise, the wife should be able to say to God, "Look, Father, at how I'm caring for this man you've entrusted to me. Look at how he's returning stepwise to the good role in creative history you gave him. He's following your Son, Jesus, and as a result is holy and blameless before you. We corule creation together, and I respect my husband's role of authority while we corule. You are his supreme authority, and he lives for your agenda here on earth. I submit to him out of respect and reverence for your excellence in creating him and giving him the kind of authority that is deserving of respect. I see him and his word and work, and I know you are worthy of all honor, praise, and glory!"

Old or new, this is the way to be human.

Kiss Me

Many years ago I wrote and recorded a song titled "Kiss Me Like a Woman."

It appeared on my *Love Life* album, a collection of songs with mostly male-female relationship themes. When I first played the recording for the record label, they struggled with whether to release it. Could I retool it a bit with some different songs, they wondered?

Amy Grant had released the album *Heart in Motion* earlier that year, and several of the songs were jetting up the pop charts, including "Every Heartbeat," a song I had helped to write. Amy had recorded mostly love songs on the album and was receiving criticism from all corners of the American evangelical community. I had nowhere near the credibility or popularity that Amy possessed. Releasing my CD to an already hostile market looked like a big risk for the record label. But after much discussion and some expert witness from Josh McDowell, the label decided that the combination of music and lyric in *Love Life* was exactly what the community needed to hear.

As they say in the South, "bless their hearts." I'll never forget my friend and label head Bill Hearn sheepishly telling me that a whole chain of stores had sent my albums back with a note to him directly: "When Charlie Peacock starts making Christian music again," the note read, "we'll start selling it."

Some stores held on to *Love Life* but initiated a policy of keeping it under the counter. This made it available to adults but kept it out of the hands of curious teens and unsuspecting children. The problem focused on the lyrics of "Kiss Me Like a Woman." What kind of lyrics could make followers of Jesus so wary, upset, and unsupportive?

> Hello baby, this is your lover speaking, just as I promised you
> I've been saving my affections for the beauty of one
> One more time show me how love is done
> Before we set the house on fire, let's take the time to build desire
> Kiss me like a woman and I'll love you like a man
> We can lie naked and unashamed, made one by divine connection
> It's good to know there's a sacred trust when you give away your
>   affections
> It's a beautiful place to be when you can trust each other completely
> Kiss me like a woman and I'll love you like a man.[1]

Some followers of Jesus wonder why musicians would think it necessary to write these kinds of lyrics. They're not alone in their wonderment. We've told and lived such small stories in front of the watching world that even they wonder why we enter the public square with this kind of artistic dialogue. When Sixpence None the Richer had their breakout hit with, ironically enough, a song titled "Kiss Me," the mainstream press took notice. *Look,* the press wrote, *they're abandoning their God songs for love songs. What a curious thing. What possible authentic interest do these artists have in such a topic?* Answer: *They're simply suppressing their Victorian impulses to achieve popular success and infiltrate the devil's playground of pop music.*

English literary journalist A. C. Grayling says that "a major source of hostility to sex is religion." He quotes Nietzsche: "Christianity gave eros poison to drink."[2]

It's all very frustrating, but I took special exception to a *Wall Street Journal* article with this tone and shot off a letter to the editor.

Dear Editor, regarding your article of April 23, 1999, titled
"Singing Songs of Love, Not God":

While the idea of a Christian singing love songs might be inconsis-
tent with the ideology of much of the contemporary Christian
music industry and its supporters, it is an idea perfectly consistent
with the Bible (see Song of Solomon). Unfortunately, this truth
and similar ones seem to find little acceptance within the Christian
music community. As a result, Christian pop music has too often
represented to the watching world a ridiculously truncated view of
what it means to be a student-follower of Jesus. There are true
artists such as Sixpence None the Richer who are trying (through
their music and lives) to remedy this error. In contradiction to
what your article intimated, artists such as these are not interested
in creating "God-free content." They are interested in creating
truthful and artful lyrics which represent their belief that all of life
is lived out before the loving gaze of God—including kisses
"beneath the milky twilight." The bottom line is this: Christians
actually enjoy kissing. It's no wonder some want to sing about it.

The Song of Solomon, or Song of Songs, is a beautiful book. It is part of
what is considered Jewish Wisdom Literature. You find it in the section of
the Bible where the Psalms and Proverbs are. Song of Songs is the best
name for the book. Whenever you see this kind of repetition in the Story,
it sends a strong signal. Think Lord of Lords and King of Kings. The repetition is about supremacy and excellence.

The cast of characters in the Song of Songs story is the lover (male),
the beloved (female), and the friends (women of Jerusalem) representing
the community. Like so much of great art, it works on several levels. This
is a story about earthly lovers, but it is also an allegory where Messiah is

the lover and the church is the beloved. This way, God in his tenderness speaks his Word in beauty and truth to all people, including those who may remain single for this lifetime.

In the story it's the female who speaks first, expressing her love to the male and desiring his love in return.

> Let him kiss me with the kisses of his mouth—
> for your love is more delightful than wine.
> Pleasing is the fragrance of your perfumes;
> your name is like perfume poured out.
> No wonder the maidens love you!
> Take me away with you—let us hurry!
> Let the king bring me into his chambers.
> We rejoice and delight in you;
> we will praise your love more than wine.
> How right they are to adore you! (Song of Songs 1:2-4)

All throughout the Song of Songs, the woman is portrayed as equal to her lover, and she speaks with the assurance that they are on level ground together. This confidence in equality is the way Jesus people are meant to follow today as well. Male and female bear the image of God and have received the rightness of Messiah that saves them in the world for kingdom work and heavenly hope.

The love of man and woman is to be sensuous. That is, love should awaken the senses. In the Song you see how love is about good tastes and smells, ones that bring pleasure. This is passionate love, not detached shopping for the best mate available for the least amount of pain.

There is a legendary story in our home and smaller tribe about a wonderful friend of ours who had fallen for a young woman at the Art House one evening. He carefully and effectively went about wooing her through good humor and gentle courtship. Everything was very studied and in its place. He was clearly passionate about the young woman, but cautiously reserved in her presence.

One day he came to me expressing his confusion about where the relationship was headed and if the woman was actually seriously interested or not. I asked him, "Do you love her?"

"Well, I really respect her," he answered.

"Yes," I said, "but do you love her?"

"I really like spending time with her," he said.

"Okay," I answered, "but do you love her?"

"Our friendship is deepening all the time."

"Yes, yes, but do you love her?"

Finally, his composure broke and passion surfaced. "Yes," he yelled. "I love her!"

"Then grab her and kiss her—let her know."

He came back the next day with a grin on his face. "You were right," he said. "That's what I needed to do."

They've been married for quite a while now and have two young boys. By all accounts they are deeply in love, telling a good story with their life.

I wasn't right, at least not by clever thinking. The Story is right. Sometimes followers of Jesus suffer from a passion deficit, or better put, a passion suppression or misdirection. We can speak and act in such a way that our community and the watching world think it would be strange for us to get excited about such things as human beauty and attraction. It shouldn't be strange; it's God's way of being human, ordained by him for his people. Why would anyone want to follow Jesus if it means being less human? To promote that people become less human is to be anti-Artist.

In the Song of Songs the lover is the one who is known and appreciated. His name and reputation is built on good storied living. Because he has a good story, it brings the community pleasure to tell good stories about him. This is also the Jesus way and the new way to be human.

Still, lovers have an idealized vision of one another. After a while this usually begins to irritate those close to the lovers. The community sees the discrepancy between the real and the ideal. In the Song, the lover's vision is actually a peek into the way God sees his people in Messiah Jesus. Hebrews 10:14 reminds us that "by one sacrifice he [Jesus] has made perfect forever those who are being made holy." Powerful romantic love is eschatological in nature. It allows people, for a slice of time, to see another human being in the light of excellent re-creation. I believe this is a common grace God has worked into the in-between times.

The lover's vision can't be sustained though. If it could, there would be no need for the Messiah. Sin and pain will find us and undo us again and again. Not to worry though; sin is clearly not the new way. The rightness and brightness of God is. We can say that something is wrong, all the while knowing and living by the truth that something is eternally right. Fueled by faith and hope, we rise each day to receive tender mercy. Through God's good gifts, especially faith, we intentionally spark the lover's vision. This is not teeth-clenched labor, but cooperation with the Spirit of God in the world. The lover's vision is a way of seeing. It's for all of God's people, toward all God's people, those named and those yet to be named, in physical and spiritual birth.

<hr />

Song of Songs is a picture of God's ways. It is a royal romance any way you look at it. Both man and woman are cogovernors of God's creation. As active participants in the kingdom way, they are coheirs with King Jesus. It is Jesus and his bride, the people of God.

When the woman says of her lover, "no wonder the maidens love you" (Song of Songs 1:3), we learn something about living in community. Friends and family hold the power of blessing in their words. Lovers gain confidence by having their love and compatibility communally confirmed. After getting to know Mark, our daughter's future husband, we said to

Molly, "No wonder you love Mark." With our son, Sam, and his future wife, Meg, it was the same. "Sam," we said, "no wonder you love Meg."

We all question our attractiveness, and the woman in the Song is no different. She thinks the sun has made her skin too dark. Never does she question her lover's attractiveness though. The lover's ideal won't let her—yet. This is how we are, as individuals and as the gathered people of God. God finds us so much more attractive than we do ourselves. If only we could see ourselves as he sees us.

Yet we can—in the Story and experientially through love. We are all new creations, sons and daughters of God through Jesus (see 2 Corinthians 5:17; Galatians 3:26). Lovers build up each other and cultivate the way of seeing that's linked to the new creation. Lovers not only build each other up with words but with imagination and creativity as well. Lovers should be like artists painting on each other the masterpieces of their hope.

The lovers in the Song of Songs have a soul love that is deep and wide. They love with their whole selves, including all their appetites and desires, physical and spiritual. Their words reveal their intimacy and closeness; these people are companions and friends. When they are apart, they carry with them the memory of each other—sight, hearing, smell, touch, and taste. It's imprinted on their souls. This is why adultery and promiscuity (physical and mental) are so harmful to people. Through unfaithfulness we make a memory of things that should not be. This memory is like nuclear waste. But rather than burying it deep within ourselves, we give it to Jesus. He has shown himself to be in complete control of matter and nonmatter, the seen and unseen. We trust him to rid the world of this waste and make us clean and new. In Jesus, no memory can keep us from the love of God and a life lived for him (see Hebrews 9:14; Jeremiah 33:8). Our work is to give and entrust the memory to him, a thousand times a thousand if that's what it takes.

As love grows and develops, lovers become more open and direct about expressing their love. This is why love between man and woman has a rhythm and a tempo. As the Song says, "Do not arouse or awaken love until it so desires" (2:7). Don't go too fast; the perfect pace is my sister, my bride—my brother, my bridegroom. You see this same progression with Jesus and his followers—my friend, my bride.

Awakening love before it's time can have painful and lasting consequences. This is especially true when we give our bodies away outside of marriage celebration and commitment. In the film *That Thing You Do,* actress Liv Tyler plays Faye, girlfriend of Jimmy, the lead singer of The Wonders. Their relationship is one-sided and headed for failure. Faye is weary from competing with Jimmy's music. In a memorable and emotional scene she confronts Jimmy with these words: "I have wasted thousands and thousands of kisses on you—kisses that I thought were special because of your lips and your smile and all your color and life. I used to think that was the real you, when you smiled. But now I know you don't mean any of it. You just save it for all your songs. Shame on me for kissing you with my eyes closed so tight."[3]

Faye's blind trust led to kisses of shame. God's way of love calls for a sacred trust built on his divine connection. Only from this starting point are we safe to risk giving away our affections. Only in him do we have the hope of being naked and unashamed.

The poetry of the Song points to a way of being human that is worth taking notice of. The words are nothing less than erotic, that is, they spark sexual desire. The words are always real. For example, are men attracted to breasts of all sizes and shapes? History and personal knowledge tell us yes. The Song of Songs not only refuses to deny this, it promotes it. It tells the truth about what it means to be a man without the world's gross immodesty. The poetry protects the mystery. Every loving follower of Jesus ought to join this work. The whole tribe of Jesus—poet regents.

Unlike the words and images heard and seen in our world today, the sex language and images of the Song of Songs are able to spark moral desire as well. This keeps the whole exchange real, just as God designed. The creational and relational must be held together for the full art of humanness to be experienced, even in matters of sexuality. There's no true enjoyment of the creation (each other's bodies) without relationship with God and engagement with his relational will. Whenever we exploit the creation without the undergirding of God's relational will, we injure ourselves and others. This is true across the spectrum of experience, but especially so with addictions.

Because of the degree of sexual damage followers carry, and the insufficient teaching they've received, discussing sex can be difficult. When I released the song "Kiss Me Like a Woman," I received an education. Seeing the pain and discomfort that a little pop song could stir created empathy in me. Sexual wounds run deep because good sexual love is meant to run deep. Beauty and shame, mystery and pain, they swim the same deep channel.

Marriage as the World-Changing Art of God

What you do with your sexuality is, from a biblical perspective, always more than a private, personal thing. It has widespread social implications. The woman belongs to the man and the man to the woman. This changes all other personal relationships. It changes the world.

In the Song of Songs, a community of people watches and encourages the lovers. The poetry calls them "the daughters of Jerusalem" and the "friends." Their presence teaches us that marriage is a public act.

The Song of Songs is a mirror of the marriage illustration of Jesus and his people. God has a role for each person in his kingdom drama, which is why a marriage should be a festive celebration of the Art of God. A marriage should say to the world, "Look at God's brilliance! Look at how he tells beautiful stories through broken people!" Followers of Jesus shouldn't hide their love and story. Storied living, empowered by love, makes the world a more beautiful place to be. It sends out an invitation to stand in its light. It whispers, *"God is, and he is among people caring for their every good need."*

In our earliest days of following Jesus, Andi and I had no idea that a marriage could aspire to something so grand and beautiful. Considering our history together, how could we? Like so many before us, this was our story before Jesus called us to follow him:

1. Boy wants to meet girl in hopes that the meeting will eventually lead to sex.
2. Girl wants to meet boy in hopes of finding a good boy.
3. Girl meets boy—boy appears to be good.
4. Boy and girl fall in love and awaken desire. Now good boy wants sex.
5. Sex leads to lying to parents and lies lead to mistrust and a break with the family.
6. Boy and girl marry young—after all, it's as if they're married already.
7. Marriage costs money; boy and girl do work that makes them miserable.
8. Boy and girl have babies and love them.
9. Babies cost even more; boy and girl work harder to get more money.
10. Boy and girl are unhappy, have less sex, and fight more. Each wonders, *Did I marry the wrong person?*

Add alcohol and drug abuse, infidelity, radical feminism, abuse, and the controlling stories within our families to this list, and it describes our experience and understanding of relationship and marriage before following Jesus.

When we stepped into the Story as active participants, this is the defining story we stepped out of. It wasn't a clean break though. It never is. Old stories die hard. They live to inform the present, no matter how erroneous or painful they may be. Some of you will read this and say, "Thank God that never happened to us." Of course some of you will recognize your story in all or part of ours. If not, you still have stories that shape your understanding of love, marriage, and life itself.

Out of our controlling story we joined up with a community of Jesus followers and watched and listened as they modeled marriage for us. Our lives had been so out of control that every good clue, no matter how small, was received with gratitude. In the beginning we were too wounded by sin to understand the huge mission God had invited us to be part of (even if some were trying to communicate it). We needed triage before we could walk, let alone sprint. Balancing a checkbook, washing clothes, and keeping a car running were major accomplishments for us. Thankfully, God's people were there to help. Our first pastor's wife, Laura, gave Andi help in the basics of organizing a home (I should have studied with her as well). A marriage class helped us with finances, communication, and sex. God's people gave concrete direction and practical help to our starving marriage and family. We eagerly studied the Story with other followers. As we received God's relational Word, it graciously began to shape and redirect us.

At that time the invitation to Christian community was about getting people saved, married or not. Once saved, it was the new follower's work to see that other people were saved. Many were convinced that our generation would see the return of Jesus, and soon. Time was running out. While people talked excitedly about the return of Jesus and the end times, I was just glad to be alive and given a second chance at living. For the first time in my adult life, I was putting aside my selfish desires to care for Andi and the children. I found new meaning and purpose and worked very hard. Andi did as well. Her words tell our story best.

> We were coming out of a chaotic life, the result of our first seven years of marriage. As the image of God in me was stirred, I wanted to shape beauty and order from our chaos....
>
>   With a clear mind and a new sense of purpose, Chuck was taking every opportunity to earn money and repair the state of our finances. As a musician, this meant that he was often gone at night and on weekends, in the studio or traveling for gigs. So I learned to take care of the bookkeeping and paperwork generated by his self-employment. As I also learned to run a household and care for

two small children, I found myself working harder than I ever had before....

Life in Christ was like breathing new air. Our household came alive. Chuck and I were working together for the preservation of our family, and individual rights could no longer be the driving force behind our choices.[1]

We both picked up good ideas from our new community about marriage (and work within marriage). But it wasn't until we read the books of Edith and Francis Schaeffer that we began to dream of marriage as a divine covenant with dynamic spiritual and social significance. When this comprehensive view began emerging, it was easier to know its presence than to describe it with words.

First, we saw how a marriage could shape for good the children who live within it. Then we saw how just one marriage can alter a neighborhood, a city, a state, a country, the world. For the first time we understood that marriage is a public act with very public consequences.

Marriage could and should change culture. How it changes it is up to the bride and bridegroom by how they love and live, not just in the bedroom but in view of the world. This is why weddings are considered legal matters and why they have witnesses. Marriage is not meant to be a private union of two lovers who hide out from the world in their protected enclave. A good marriage should be the Art of God in the world pointing to his existence, care, and excellence. Marriage is storytelling and storied living.

These ideas came to Andi and me in digestible pieces like messages in a bottle, one word at a time floating in the ocean of our hearts and beaching on the surface of our thoughts. Little by little we began to speak them and act them—word and work.

Most of the tribal teaching on marriage, especially the evangelical variety, never gets to the world-changing Art of God I've just hinted at. Instead, our tribal teachers and writers give practical help for everyday life within a much smaller agreed-upon context. For Americans, that context is the word and work within the American dream long before it's the Word and work of God, people, and place, where people live entirely for God under his ways of being human.

The presence of popular ideas and story lines in the marketplace is an indicator of what people assign importance to. A quick glance at Christian periodicals for men, women, and marriage will reveal the kind of practical help people want, and which areas of interest are salable to professing Christians. I recently found articles in a marriage magazine on having fun together doing spring cleaning, on the effect of TV viewing on marriage, on improving your attitude about finances, and on men who want to "just do it" and women who "feel rushed."

A men's online magazine included articles on when and where a quiet time is best, on winning and keeping your little girl's heart, on overcoming secret sin such as bitterness and pornography, on learning to communicate with women, and on how to tell if your child is abusing drugs.

A women's magazine included articles on gaining the respect of a stepdaughter, on controlling anger, and on getting much-needed girl time with friends.

Other teachers and writers direct followers to the Bible for a foundational theology of marriage. A theology of marriage is human reflection on the Story in relationship to marriage. Most theologies of marriage begin and end with Genesis 2:24, Matthew 19:6, and 1 Corinthians 13. Even if you don't recognize these references, you know the words. Anyone who has ever attended a marriage ceremony will recognize them. Marriage and sex: "They will become one flesh." Divorce: "What God has joined together, let man not separate." And, the way of love: "Love is patient, love is kind. It does not envy, it does not boast, it is not proud. It is not rude, it is not self-seeking, it is not easily angered, it keeps no record of wrongs. Love does not delight in evil but rejoices with the truth. It always protects, always trusts, always hopes, and always perseveres."

Though the Word is strong, a theology is only as strong as the place the human knower stands or the lens he or she looks through. Individuals and institutionalized gatherings of followers look at the Bible from various viewpoints. These viewpoints affect theologies of marriage. Most of the energy of these theologies is spent on the issue of gender roles in family, society, and the church. *Very little attention is given to the married couple as a strategic, entrusted, and equipped team after the pattern of the first man and woman.*

Early on in their romance, before marriage, our daughter and son-in-law gave themselves a name: Team 35. The naming set the tone for their marriage. It reminded them—we're a team. Today their marriage tells a story that they work together in the world, carrying out the King's agenda. By all accounts they yield to a controlling Story larger than any other stories within them or around them. In short, they're interested in the same things Jesus is interested in.

This idea cuts to the heart of what defines marriage for those who profess to follow Jesus. Does the marriage say to the community and the world, "We are a team, committed to each other and whoever or whatever Jesus is committed to. In as much as we're married to each other, we're married to him first, to his ways, to his agenda in the world. We let no other story control our ways but his. We are grateful to follow him and serve together as coheirs of life."

If this hints at the way marriage is to intersect with the new way to be human, and I believe it does, is this what we tell young followers marriage is? Is this what Christian parents teach their children? Is this what the watching world thinks of when they think of marriage and the followers of Jesus? I wonder if so-called Christian marriages are constructed to be interested in the same things Jesus is interested in? Or have we shaped them to fit the interests of a smaller, socially agreed-upon context?

Consider Brian and Kelly, parents of two (and for our purposes, a composite couple). Let's ask them some questions. Brian and Kelly, tell us about following Jesus and how following him affects your day-to-day life.

> We're Christians and have been for a long time. We are committed to Christian beliefs and values. We've received Jesus Christ as our personal Savior and have convinced others of the need for Jesus in their own lives. We believe that Christianity is important for moral guidance and fellowship with like-minded people—people who value what's good and right. We're very profamily. We try to be good witnesses in our community and in the workplace by doing good work and treating people well. Both of us are involved in Monday morning devotionals with other Christians at our places of work. And of course we fellowship at a local Bible-believing church. Our kids are involved in youth group, and we give to a number of ministries in addition to supporting our church. We try to work our Christianity into daily life, to be salt and light in the world. When you read the Bible, it seems like Christianity is mostly about what's to come—about God forgiving our sins so that we can be with him in heaven. We know God wants to change us now, though, so we ask for forgiveness and are always praying to become more like Jesus. So that's how it [Christianity] applies to our life right now.

Earlier we pulled back the curtain on Andi's and my life to look at our foundational stories. If we do the same with Brian and Kelly's life, we'd see they embody the following stories:

1. *Have as much fun as possible when you're a kid.* For Brian, a good southern boy, this meant sowing a few wild oats. Play with sin, but don't let it have you. Kelly, simply put, is a good girl and always has been.

2. *At some point, take care of sin.* This was especially important for
   Brian due to his previously noted teenage sins. Brian was raised
   to believe that only through Jesus can a person know forgiveness of sin and receive eternal life. He confessed his sin and
   need of a Savior when he was sixteen. Kelly received Jesus
   Christ as her personal Savior when she was five years old and
   has believed in Jesus for as long as she can remember.

3. Both Brian and Kelly received good grades throughout school.
   In high school each worked toward academic and sports schol-
   arships. Their individual goals were to attend the right university, graduate, and find a job that paid well.

4. Both Brian and Kelly set out to marry someone of the wife or
   husband variety—a good girl or good boy, not a bad girl or bad
   boy one sows wild oats with. Brian kept his wild side to himself
   until two years after he and Kelly were married. (This confession caused some initial problems, but counseling helped.)

5. Today Brian and Kelly work very hard to ensure that their
   family is as well off or better than their own families of origin.
   They own a beautiful home in a safe neighborhood.

6. They raise their children in a Christian environment of home,
   school, sports, and church activities. They work at providing
   their children with ample opportunities to receive Jesus Christ
   as their personal Savior. They've heard it said that it takes as
   many as ten to twelve times of hearing the gospel before a person accepts it.

7. Though their children are still in elementary school, Brian and
   Kelly are thinking ahead to the day their children will attend
   university. Because of this, grades are taken very seriously in
   their home. After their children graduate from high school,
   Brian and Kelly will strongly encourage them to study for an
   employable profession. Once out of college, they want their

kids to be safe and sound in well-paying jobs. Finally, their hope is for their children to marry other good, highly motivated kids from reputable, godly families. Far off in the distance, they look forward to being grandparents, but only if their children are settled down and financially prepared.

This is Brian and Kelly's controlling story. It's a complex mass of facts, values, cares, and commitments. It defines life and provides them with time-consuming work. When Brian and Kelly are not working long and hard at their demanding jobs or raising their family, they enjoy hobbies such as golf and antiquing. There's time for dinner with friends, a movie or a sporting event, a special midnight Christmas Eve service, a worthy fund-raiser, or a weekend working on a Habitat for Humanity house.

For our imaginary friends Brian and Kelly, this is married life, and a very full married life it is. For Brian and Kelly, this is what it means to know the King's agenda and carry it out with like-minded people. This is what it means for them to change culture through marriage, to play their role in the kingdom drama. Though they would never describe it in these terms, this is what they're doing on some level. Isn't it? If they're not modeling for the watching world the Art of God, if they're not sending out an invitation to stand in his light, if they're not saying, "Look at God, isn't he brilliant? Look at what he does in people yielded to his will" just what exactly are they saying and doing? What is their word and work?

When a couple says they're committed to Christian beliefs and values, does it mean they're committed to losing their lives? Does it mean that they will set aside all their ideas about what makes up a life in exchange for God's ways of being human? Are they saying they will follow Jesus everywhere he leads them?

When a couple says they've each received Jesus Christ as their personal Savior and have convinced others of the need for Jesus in their own lives, what do they think he saved them from? What did he save them to? More to the point, what exactly do they think God is doing right now in redemption through his Son, Jesus? And if they can locate the answer, how are they living in cooperation with it? How does their word and work match up with the agenda of God in the world?

When a couple says they believe that Christianity is important for moral guidance and fellowship with like-minded people—people who value what's good and right—how do they reconcile all the time their Teacher spent with people so unlike himself, people who were not good and right?

All these questions are the offspring of the mother of all questions every couple faces: What story defines our marriage?

⇌

In *Life After God,* author Douglas Coupland shares the following exchange with his mother regarding the defining story of her marriage.

"She says: 'First there is love, then there is disenchantment and then there is the rest of your life.'

"And I say, 'But what *about* the rest of your life—what about all the time that remains?'

"And she says, 'Oh—there's friendship. Or at least familiarity. And there's safety. And after that there's sleep.'

"I think to myself: How do any of us know that it's going to end up like this? That *this* is all there was maybe going to be? I say, 'Oh, God.'

"And my mother says to me, 'Honey, God is what keeps us together after the love is gone.'"[2]

When my research assistant, Jenna Galbreth, handed me this quote, she added a little commentary to it: "This is what scares people from marriage, I think." Jenna's correct. If this is a common, defining story with respect to marriage, people should stay single.

Mother Coupland's love has a season, a time that is rich and good, visceral and vibrant. This is the idealized vision of love portrayed in the Song of Songs. Earlier I made the point that powerful romantic love is eschatological in nature—it allows lovers, through common grace, to see each other in light of what they could be. When time and circumstance show this love to be what it is—an ideal—many people bail emotionally (and physically). It is simply not what they signed up for. They thought the season was the life itself. Add to this challenges, failures, suffering, and nasty surprises, and watch disenchantment bloom. In many instances, this is when marriages collapse. The love the couple knew in the beginning was so good and right, one or both of them hunger to replicate it with a new partner. The wounded couple has neither the intent nor the resources to renew love together and rebuild on a stronger foundation. Somehow it seems better to just start again. Better luck next time.

The way of Coupland's mother is not to bail, but to stay. According to her, God sustains the human relationship when passion fades. Husband and wife convert to a cozy and familiar friendship. This becomes the pattern for the rest of life. It's not exciting, but it's safe.

Brian and Kelly's story line is about God and people too, but with an emphasis on Jesus as their personal Savior. After Jesus, there are other important essentials as well, particularly the commitment to personal achievement and the American dream. They've both been taught that whether it is grades, sports, or community involvement, the formula is personal achievement equals personal reward.

The next step in the plan (and it usually *is* a plan) is to deal with the issue of aloneness. While some people marry at college, Brian and Kelly waited until graduation. Their attraction to each other was very strong, and in the most classic sense they fell deeply in love. Kelly believed that Brian was the one, the good boy that her parents had urged her to one day marry. Brian was confident that Kelly was indeed a woman of the wife variety—beautiful, smart, and godly. Both professed Christian faith and vowed to build a family based on Christian values.

After two years of marriage Kelly was shocked to discover that Brian was not a virgin when they married. Brian had sex with two different girls the summer before his junior year in high school. One got pregnant and had an abortion. This was not what Kelly had signed up for. They went to counseling together for two months. Kelly continued for a year after that. Brian wondered if their marriage would survive, but grace and time healed the wound, and life returned to normal.

Both Brian and Kelly worked long hours toward the goal of buying a new home in the Strassburg Hill subdivision on the safe side of town. Strassburg Elementary School had the best test scores in the state. Once their home was built, they began a family.

Brian's sexual past fueled their commitment to strong Christian parenting. They would make sure the children were raised in Christian environments with lots of supervision. Home became a sanctuary from the evils of the world. Christian schools provided values congruent with the home as well as with competitive sports and college prep. Their children would be given every opportunity to receive Jesus at the earliest age and to succeed at this life, living with the hope of heaven.

The story line for marriage in the new way to be human is nothing like Coupland's mother or our model Christian couple. For some readers this may be very difficult to understand. Stay with me. The kind of world-changing marriage student-followers ought to hunger for has the shape of Jesus and the kingdom.

Passionate Realism

The new way of marriage begins with the passionate love portrayed in the Song of Songs. Great art always begins with passion, and the Art of God in marriage is no different. So yes, followers of Jesus fall in love and show physical and mental enthusiasm for each other. Their passion is holistic, having both a public and private side.

There's no place for disenchantment in the new way, only realism. Of course, disenchantment occurs, but why? It's because marital expectations are disconnected from the God-human conversation. God has clearly informed his followers of their real condition. We have full disclosure regarding everyone. Jesus calls his people to be passionate realists, to carry on with enthusiasm in light of what is real. One day the passion is sexual love. Another day, it might be suffering after the way of Jesus. In everything, passion prevails. In the new way, people know they've married wounded sinners who have no chance for recovery outside the grace of God. Marriage is a covenant of two people agreeing to recover together, each in different ways at different paces, both under the tutelage of the Teacher, Jesus.

Student-followers of Jesus have fallen prey to consumer marriages and have suffered great wounds for it. The Story teaches that the effects of sin are total in scope. It also teaches the beauty and majesty of love between man and woman. Everyone who follows Jesus is asked to hold to both of these as reality.

A man shops to find the perfect woman with just the right body, intellect, and godliness. He marries her and discovers she's terrified of being left alone. It's particularly acute in bad weather. He works as a consultant to NFL franchises and travels every week. It's his dream job, and he's well paid. She wants him to work at home. He wants her to get over it.

A woman shops to find the perfect man with just the right body, intellect, and godliness. She marries him and discovers he's only mildly interested in sex. He tells her it's because of something that happened when he was young. That's all he'll say. She saved herself for marriage and looked forward to a healthy sex life with a man who adored her—body, mind, and soul. He says she's acting like a nymphomaniac. She wants him to act like a man.

In the new way of marriage, a couple is not surprised by sin and its damage. They might be surprised at how it manifests itself and the extent of its exponential impact. But they're not surprised by its presence. They know that sin is constantly mutating like a virus and re-presenting itself as something new. These new forms of sin may be unpredictable; that they're coming is not.

Nevertheless, all of us do have some predictable, sinful patterns of behavior that we return to again and again as we try to make life work apart from God. Sometimes these patterns are our best misguided attempt at a solution for a problem brought about by some other sin. Couples often coevolve in sin as each person alters his or her thinking and doing to tolerate the other's sin. A spouse who lives with an alcoholic changes her behavior to tolerate the alcoholic. She begins to make special allowances for his sin, such as having sex to shut up a drunken rant or buying the alcohol to keep him from driving to the store. What was previously unheard of becomes normal and accepted. The couple grows sicker together, moving in a negative direction. These are dramatic examples, but honestly the ones most of us know are even creepier. They're of the guerrilla warfare variety, staying in the shadows, sniping from a place of invisibility. Even professional soldiers of the heart and mind have trouble locating them.

In the new way of marriage, the couple moves together in the positive direction of wellness and rightness. This requires passionate realism. It requires honesty about what stories control us. It requires the empathy of Jesus manifest in the man and woman. Most important, marriage is a microexample of a macronecessity. Marriages are little films showing the kingdom lifestyle of forgiveness.

Consider the man who married the woman who was terrified of being left alone. What would his situation look like through the lens of the new way? Passionate realism will mean that passionate love exists. It is a reality. But so is the fact that his wife is wounded regardless of how seemingly beautiful, smart, or godly she first appeared. A passionate realist will understand this. He will continue to love while acknowledging the reality that something is clearly wrong with the person he loves. He won't be surprised by it or insensitive to her. He'll feel about sin and suffering the way Jesus does. It's not the way it's supposed to be, and thankfully there's a plan in motion to rid the world of it. With the eyes of a passionate-realist lover, he'll see in his wife both shame and glory, who she's becoming, and who she will be in perfection.

Both the man and the woman have to be honest about the stories that control them. Passionate love requires that the woman tell her story. She has to say, "Here's my story of why I'm afraid to be alone and how I think I ended up this way." Maybe some of the story makes sense and some doesn't. Maybe all she can do is identify the symptoms because she has no clue to what really ails her.

The man's job is not to fix her, but to listen with an empathetic ear. Then it's his turn to talk. He loves football. As a high-schooler he dreamed of playing cornerback for an NFL team. He could have, but his knee gave out. By consulting for NFL franchises, he's still around the game, and that's rewarding enough. He can't conceive of giving it up for what he sees as a "woman's irrational fears." The woman's task is not to enlighten her husband to the power of feelings or realign his hierarchy of meaning. Instead, she listens with an empathetic ear.

If you think reading about this makes it sound too easy, you're right. It's difficult and messy—something you might work on for a lifetime. That's the point. Love costs something—you, me.

The empathetic ear is the ear of the priestly Jesus. Pastor and theologian Daniel Doriani likes to say that Jesus is our empathetic hero, that Jesus is family. He is the representative man, and so, empathetic. Jesus is also divine, hence heroic. He is the Pioneer-Champion who shared our humanity to bring us to glory through his suffering. He has liberated us from the fear of death and the accusations of Satan. He pioneered the way in which the whole family now walks and follows. Because he himself suffered in the world and was tempted, he is able to help us with the same problems. Jesus is a faithful and merciful High Priest—one who is able to sympathize with our weaknesses, who has suffered and been tempted in every way, yet is without sin (see Hebrews 4:15).

Jesus provides everything a priest should. He is the pure sacrifice that saves, forgives, and restores completely. His work is finished. Never again does sin need to be dealt with in this way. He has provided his children with complete access to God, complete atonement for sin, and a completely clear conscience. It's at the feet of this Priest that we tell each other our stories.

This being so, when the woman tells her story, it doesn't have to threaten the man. He can say to himself, "Okay, I didn't see this coming, but I knew that something like it would come."

When the man tells his story, the woman can have a similar response. She should not be surprised that her good man is not so good after all. He should not be surprised that his beautiful wife is wounded and in need of re-creation. When what is real is allowed to surface, passion should be right there with it. Passion is the river that runs through it. Instead of passionate lovemaking, now it's passionate suffering. In all things, God's enthusiasm for his people becomes visible in the lives of lovers.

~~~~~~~

Truthfully, it's all lovemaking. The couple should lovingly care for each other as holy priests serving in acknowledgment of Jesus's finished priestly work. Sin is dealt with once for all. Followers are called to know this essential fact and pray for grace to stop living as if it isn't a fact. Forgiveness is as real as your own skin. We give our priestly energies to it and show each other empathy for weakness and the painful, shameful consequences of sin.

Married followers give each other complete access, they suffer together, and when all is revealed, they tell this story back to God in prayer, *together*. The prayer is not the man's or the woman's. It is *their* prayer. Instead of *Father, please fix my wife so I can get back to work* or *Please tell my husband that this is just who I am,* they pray to the Father: *Here we are again. It looks different than the last time, but the need is the same. We need you, Jesus. We need a fresh dose of the memory of forgiveness and your kind of rightness. We need your kingdom in us. We're lost inside ourselves, and we want to be found in you. We are naked and ashamed, and what we really want to do is reject each other and hide over in the shadows behind the trees. But you taught us to make our requests known, so here we go. We need specific help and healing in the following areas...*

Talking with God together about these matters is always a good first line of defense. He's in charge of the re-creation. It makes sense to go right to the top. Sometimes sin, particularly gross self-interest and pride, will so harden a heart that you need a jackhammer to break up the cement. When this happens, it's good for a couple to take their show on the road and make it public with someone who cares about what Jesus cares about. This could be a counselor, a psychologist, or a counseling pastor. In some marriages people are so wounded by sin that they each need a helper. Here a trained counselor-psychologist listens to stories and then reintroduces the wounded person to Jesus in every area of the person's sin and suffering.

This is, in fact, the work of the healthy marriage and the healthy church, but we have drifted so far from the Jesus model for life that we need other means of help. As always, God's grace is sufficient, and he mercifully brings people along who mirror the wounded healer to those in need of healing. If a married couple finds it difficult or even impossible to develop and implement passionate realism, they should look for this kind of help. If they can't identify or be honest about what stories control them, if they can't forgive or show empathy for sin, temptation, and weakness, they should get help in learning these vital life skills.

I'll boldly say there is no authentic marriage, following in the new way, apart from passionate realism, storytelling, empathy, and forgiveness. You can call these by other names, but their necessity and fruit is the same. If a man and woman cannot or will not wrap their hearts around them, they will suffer a loss of integrity and the gift of life that should be theirs. The refusal to be passionate, honest, empathetic, and forgiving is never a private choice. It is never just personal. A dispassionate, dishonest, non-empathetic, unforgiving person pollutes spouse, children, family, public square, nation, and world. That he or she would refuse to acknowledge the behavior and change or receive help is a baffling cruelty. That a professing follower of Jesus would consistently behave this way is scary as hell.

The refusal to embrace honesty, forgiveness, and empathy is a form of unbelief, of not trusting God with the unknown. Some people become convinced that it is better to accept the misery they do know than to trust God for something they don't know.

Yet the Story, particularly the book of Hebrews, reminds us of how future-oriented storied faith and living are. Family members, brothers and sisters who have already faithfully run the race, who have endured and persevered, stand at the finish line cheering us on, testifying to God's faithfulness. The witness message to all followers, to every marriage, is that it's God who enables us to run to the end. It's God who will help us through temptation, sin, mess, and confusion. Still, we intentionally throw off every sin that would hinder our race. Followers of Jesus identify sin, confess it, throw it away, and stay the course of life that God has given us.

One of my favorite songs is by my friend Steve Taylor. Steve clearly understands the message of the book of Hebrews.

Off in the distance
Bloodied but wise
As you squint with the light of the truth in your eyes

And I saw you
Both hands were raised
And I saw your lips move in praise
And I saw you steady your gaze
For the finish line

Every idol like dust
A word scattered them all
And I rose to my feet when you scaled the last wall
And I gasped
When I saw you fall
In his arms
At the finish line[1]

As Daniel Doriani so often says, we look to Jesus the Trailblazer, the Champion, for immediate, present help in running the race. He will carry us on to the finish. He knows the path. Even though we grow weary, we don't give up. Jesus is too near us for that. He guides us, carries us, and will receive us at the finish line.

From the beginning, man and woman were created to have a public life together in the world, caring for the world. Whether we are married or single, the new way to be human is a reinvitation to this way of living. When men and women do partner in marriage, the call is to step into the Story of God-people-and-place. This new one-flesh partnership becomes, in the world, a model of the unity of purpose the Tri-personal God knows. The heirs of the kingdom do the work of the King. If a follower of Jesus never marries, the calling is the same: Know the King's agenda and carry it out with tribes of like-minded people.

Above all, this means caring for God's relational Word and his creational Word. Because of the Creator's creational Word, man and woman can walk with the Creator on earth (his place). The Creator shares his creation with man and woman (his creative Word) and gives them the good work of caring for it. As 1 Corinthians 10:26 says, "The earth is the Lord's, and everything in it."

Marriage is two followers working together to speak and act directly for God in the world. First Peter 4:11 teaches, "If anyone speaks, he should do it as one speaking the very words of God. If anyone serves, he should do it with the strength God provides, so that in all things God may be praised through Jesus Christ." Jesus has reconnected the God-human conversation. He has cleared the lines. The only way I'll find static or distortion is if it's on my end. God never asks, "Can you hear me now?"

Marriages are to be living partnerships of the new way, making the kingdom known through kingdom living that reflects the King's rule and reign. In simplest terms, this means we are all—whether married or single—created to be interested in the same things Jesus is interested in. To have no interest is to miss what it means to be human.

⌒

The joining of man and woman together in joyful, passionate friendship and sex is just the beginning. As good as it can be, it is not the thing itself. The life of marriage partnership is everything I've been describing and more. Passion is holistic. It's about passion for God's creative and relational Word. The work that pours out from this passion is more than all the books in the world could ever hold. Nevertheless, this kind of passion does include enthusiasm for kisses and orgasms; knowing the story and creating memories of it in the world; caring for the poor, the widows, and the orphans; and imaginatively caring for everything from music and oceans to zebras and football players.

You see, boys don't have to grow up thinking that their attraction to girls is all about one day having sex with them. They could grow up with a bigger story than this. A young man could say, "I can't wait to meet the woman I will share my passion with. I can't wait to create new stories together in the context of the grand Story God is telling throughout history."

Girls don't have to grow up thinking that their worth is tied to how well they can attract and keep a boy. They, too, can grow up with a bigger story. A woman could say, "I can't wait to meet the man I will be naked and unashamed with. Together we will make love and make life, and we will follow Jesus together wherever he leads. Together we will be interested in the same things Jesus is interested in—all of his creativity and the work of restoring it to rightness."

When the time is right and desire is awakened, these followers could come together with passionate realism, story, empathy, and forgiveness and say to the world: "We don't belong here. We belong to a new world coming, one with an entirely different economy. Nevertheless, we know what to do while we're here: passionate word and work, passionate storytelling and storied living. In plenty and in want, in pleasure and in suffering, we are prepared to follow in the way of Jesus. We're prepared to become, in weakness, the Art of God in marriage. We will trust Jesus to heal our wounds, give us unceasing unity of purpose, and lead us to the finish line. And when we cross that line into the fullness of victory, we will fall on our knees, point to Jesus, and shout: 'You did it! You did it! You did it! When we were lost and without hope, with no faith that we could keep on loving each other, you did it! Thank you, Jesus. Praise you, Lord.'"

Then the heat from the glory of God will fill our bones, and we will tremble with the sheer pleasure of being known completely, without shame or guilt of any kind.

Making the New
Way Visible

Work, Money, and the Kiss of God

God appointed the first man and woman as caretakers of his creative and relational Word. When Jesus arrived on earth as the Word made flesh, he nuanced this stewardship role. He announced that the time had come for a new opportunity: the kingdom of God. Everyone who followed him and obeyed his commandments would have a place in his kingdom. We're still called to care for the Father's creativity, but the relational Word is now summed up in " 'Love the Lord your God with all your heart and with all your soul and with all your strength and with all your mind'; and, 'love your neighbor as yourself' " (Luke 10:27). These words play host to the controlling Story behind all our creative work. Obedience to this summation of God's will is what it means to take God's Word very seriously.

In the new way to be human, the knowledge and practice of work begins with four simple ideas:

1. My work is storytelling and storied living after the pattern of Jesus. This means knowing and telling the Story and making God's reign and rule visible in daily life. It means overcoming evil with good and pushing back the effects of the Fall.

2. My work ought to be inescapably connected to the Father's business in the world, cooperating with him in restoring rightness, doing justice, and showing mercy. This means removing any impairment to healthy functioning.

3. My work is to care for God's creativity—people and place and all of creation. This means dreaming well for it and using creation for the good of people and to proclaim God's excellence as Creator.

4. My work is to care for God's relational will, to know it, teach it to others, and embody it. More than anything, this means loving God with my whole being, and loving my neighbor with the kind of love and care I desire. It means doing for others what God has so graciously done for me.

This is my work. It's the work of anyone following Jesus. It's the work of individuals and the work of marriages. At the end of Robert Bellah's classic *Habits of the Heart,* he raises a plea for the transformation of work so that it becomes "a contribution to the good of all and not merely as a means to one's advancement."[1] This is a view of work congruent with the new way.

There's a story of three great medieval stone masons and a visitor who watched their work with interest.

"What are you doing?" the visitor asked the first mason.

"I'm cutting stone," the mason replied.

A second mason chimed in, "I'm making a living."

"And how about you?" the visitor asked the third man.

"Me? I'm building a cathedral for God and his people."[2]

Each mason did the same work but with vastly different motivation and ideas about the nature of their work. The first mason focused on the individual task of cutting stone. Though practical, his vision of work was very small and individualized. The second mason focused on the compensation he received for his labor. His work was a means to an end: money. The third mason worked for the good of people and the glory of God. He received compensation, but it's not his starting place for thinking about work. This is also a view of work congruent with the new way.

Work is connected to telling a good story with your life. The goal of work is faithfulness to God, people, and place. Any work that accomplishes this is work worth pursuing and doing.

⁓

Do you remember how I described my marriage before following Jesus? Andi and I found out that being married was more costly than being single, so we worked for money in jobs that made us miserable. Then the children came and we needed more money, so we worked even harder. I wanted to get paid for making music but often had to take other work instead—usually minimum-wage labor in food service. Even some of the music work I got made me miserable. Why? I did very bad music for money.

We had no role models near us or clues that work could be anything other than something you didn't want to do but had to do in order to earn money. I had been very self-absorbed as a young husband and father. It wasn't until I was clean and sober that I contributed to our family budget with anything like faithfulness. Even then my focus was on getting the money.

Remember the composite Christian couple Brian and Kelly? Their goal as young people was to attend the right university, graduate, and find a job that paid well. Their goal as parents was to see that their children studied for an employable profession. They could see being grandparents one day, but only if their children were settled down and financially prepared. Here, too, money was the focus.

You might be saying to yourself, "Hey, that's my focus too and what's wrong with it?" What's wrong is that the focus exists because of something other than God and his ways. It's a prison for the mind. At Leavenworth or San Quentin, cannabis or cigarettes are the prison currency. In the prison of the mind, it's money. Mary Pipher writes that "we all suffer from existential flu as we search for meaning in a culture that values money, not meaning. Everyone I know wants to do good work. But right now we have an enormous gap between doing what's meaningful and doing what is reimbursed."[3] Many citizens, including followers of Jesus, have done away with the gap altogether and have learned to say, "Show me the money." The money is the meaning.

Prisons of the mind are always in development and manufacture, but so is the historical conversation concerning them. Going back several centuries, John Winthrop (1588–1649) defined *success* not as material wealth but as "the creation of a community in which genuinely ethical and spiritual life could be lived."[4] Benjamin Franklin (1706–1790), on the other hand, gave "classic expression to what many felt in the eighteenth century—and many have felt ever since—to be the most important thing about America: the chance for the individual to get ahead on his own initiative."[5] This became known as utilitarian individualism. The idea being that if a society will allow each person the freedom to pursue his or her own interests, the social good will automatically emerge. Utilitarian individualism (in its worst forms) saw opposition by the mid-nineteenth century. Women, clergy, poets, and writers raised objections to a life lived in pursuit of material gain. People still raise objections today, but their voices are mice in a world of elephants.

One voice that is not small is the voice of Jesus. I'll share with you something I believe he told me regarding work and money. My confidence that this came from Jesus is found in a promise he made to his followers. He said, "But the Counselor, the Holy Spirit, whom the Father will send in my name, will teach you all things and will remind you of everything I have said to you" (John 14:26). Now I don't know why, but when I hear from Jesus in this way, he always calls me Chuck.

"Chuck, this is Jesus speaking. 'I tell you, do not worry about your life, what you will eat or drink; or about your body, what you will wear' (Matthew 6:25).

"Chuck, you cannot be the servant of both God and things on earth. It's futile to have two ultimate goals or points of reference for your actions.

You already recognize that one must become subordinate to the other. You can plainly see that you truly cannot serve two masters—their requirements conflict. When the treasures of the heart are not the treasures of God, your life becomes an endless cycle of pursuing financial security and living to please man, doesn't it? This is the futile life" (see Matthew 6:24).

I thought a bit on my own for a moment. *Yes, I can serve material goods, value them, care for them, and use them well for God's kingdom purposes. Since I know this and understand the call of stewardship, I'll hold on to this truth and let go of everything that doesn't fit within what faith allows or requires of me.*

"Chuck, 'I have often told you before and now say again even with tears, many live as enemies of the cross of Christ. Their destiny is destruction, their god is their stomach, and their glory is in their shame. Their mind is on earthly things. But our citizenship is in heaven' (Philippians 3:18-20).

" 'Rejoice in the Lord always. I will say it again: Rejoice! Let your gentleness be evident to all. The Lord is near. Do not be anxious about anything, but in everything, by prayer and petition, with thanksgiving, present your requests to God. And the peace of God, which transcends all understanding, will guard your hearts and your minds in Christ Jesus' (Philippians 4:4-7).

"You can work hard and you can care about your loved ones, your family. But don't be anxious—not even about caring for them. Remember what 1 Timothy 6:6-12 says: 'But godliness with contentment is great gain. For we brought nothing into the world, and we can take nothing out of it. But if we have food and clothing, we will be content with that. People who want to get rich fall into temptation and a trap and into many foolish and harmful desires that plunge men into ruin and destruction. For the love of money is a root of all kinds of evil. Some people, eager for money, have wandered from the faith and pierced themselves with many griefs. But you [Chuck], man of God, flee from all this, and pursue righteousness, godliness, faith, love, endurance and gentleness. Fight the good fight of the faith. Take hold of the eternal life to which you were called when you made your good confession in the presence of many witnesses.'"

That's it, I thought to myself. *Don't hold it lightly. Don't be tentative. Hold it as you would anything of great value.*

"Chuck, don't put your 'hope in wealth, which is so uncertain,' but put your 'hope in God, who richly provides us with everything for our enjoyment' (1 Timothy 6:17). Just 'do good.' In fact, be 'rich in good deeds...generous and willing to share' (verse 18). If you will live this way, you 'will lay up treasure for [yourself] as a firm foundation for the coming age, so that you may take hold of the life that is truly life' (verse 19).

"Chuck, work. And while you work here on earth, do not worry about things on earth. Instead, seek the kingdom first and always first. When you get up in the morning think about the kingdom. From now on, make it your top priority to identify and involve yourself only in what God is doing and in the kind of rightness he has. Everything else you need will be provided (see Matthew 6:33).

"Chuck, remember that a friend of the world is an enemy of God (see James 4:4), in fact, a hater of God. This is why you can't claim to love God and then turn and return to loving something he does not love. A lover of God will love what God loves and hate what he hates.

"Finally, Chuck, 'whatever is true, whatever is noble, whatever is right, whatever is pure, whatever is lovely, whatever is admirable—if anything is excellent or praiseworthy—think about such things. Whatever you have learned or received or heard from me, or seen in me—put it into practice. And the God of peace will be with you'" (Philippians 4:8-9).

Jesus communicates with his people. "My sheep," Jesus says, "listen to my voice; I know them, and they follow me" (John 10:27). He speaks in sheeply ways that sheep can understand. On the subject of work and money, he gave me important words from the Story, beginning with his own. My journal reflections on what I was hearing have stood the test of congruency. They send a strong memory that God spoke and I responded. (Jesus even used a little Dallas Willard, a good teacher in the here and now, to make the teaching as clear as glass to a dim soul like me.)

Do people need a means of exchange for goods and services in the world? Of course, and God knows this. But neither the need for money nor the need for goods and services defines work for the man or woman following in the new way. Here we need the long memory about what happened in Eden. The gathered tribe of Jesus is meant to be a people who take God's relational Word seriously. "All that we are and do as Christians is based upon the one-off unique achievement of Jesus. It is because he inaugurated the kingdom that we can live the kingdom."[6] The kingdom Jesus announced did create a new world and context, and a new world would require a new way of being human. Jesus came announcing a kingdom that must "overturn all other agendas."[7] This includes our agendas regarding work, money, success, peace and safety, and the goals we instill in our children.

Can it really be that our work is to do good and that's all? Yes. The simplest theology I can give is do good work and trust God to provide. This is the old way of Eden made new through Jesus. Honestly, this is just too good to be true for most followers, and so in matters of work and money, we think and behave as practical atheists. This is why followers like Brian and Kelly are the rule and not the exception. Rather than trusting God's relational Word, we trust our own ambitions.

All God wants is a people who will do their work as unto him, for his kingdom purposes, and trust him to care for what he loves. If we have a need for resources to accomplish good, he wants us to talk to him about it. If the work we want to do really *is* good, we can trust that he is way ahead of us. His whole re-creation project is about what is good and right. His invitation is to get in step with his goodness and rightness.

The book of James asks, "What causes fights and quarrels among you? Don't they come from your desires that battle within you? You want something but don't get it. You kill and covet, but you cannot have what you want. You quarrel and fight. You do not have, because you do not ask God. When you ask, you do not receive, because you ask with wrong motives, that you may spend what you get on your pleasures" (4:1-3).

How do God's people drift so far from the shore? Craig Gay says that the drift is a result of our imaginations, "that we imagine our world in such a way that we ignore the real reality of God's gracious presence within it."[8] When the Story speaks of "the world," it defines it in three ways: (1) the earth as a place created by the Creator, (2) all the people groups of creation, and (3) all the ways contrary to God's ways. This last definition is the world people imagine. It's not the world of God and his ways of being human in the world.

The mother of Jesus spoke of God saying, "He has scattered the proud in the imagination of their hearts." (Luke 1:51, RSV). Every follower must wrestle with the question, Am I of the scattering or the gathering? First Peter 5:5 reminds me, "God opposes the proud but gives grace to the humble."

⁓

It's ironic that at this very moment I need to stop writing to make a phone call. A music colleague offered me some work yesterday, and I need to tell him thanks but no thanks. Writing this chapter and rereading the words that Jesus loaned me some time ago helped me make a decision. I have lots of good work in front of me to do, work that I'm confident Jesus wants me involved in. On the other hand, I'm not at all confident that the work offered by my friend is something I'm supposed to do. If I were to do it, it would be for the money alone.

It's not that there isn't good to do inside the work being offered. And it's not that I couldn't earn the money and do good with it. But if I stop the good I'm doing to go pick up a check, it's like telling Jesus, "Just in case you don't take care of me, I know I'll have this money to fall back on." Don't think I haven't done this before. I have. And every single time it's like putting money in a purse with holes in it. I'm learning to give careful thought to my ways and ask if my ways are God's ways.

I submit to God and resist the devil and his prison. While the devil runs in one direction, I run to Jesus. He's running right toward me too, carrying a big bucket of holy water. He pours it on me, purifying my heart and hands. He takes my double mind, and with a tender squeeze makes it one with his. I'm completely undone by this gift. I grieve my sin and cry as if death has crept down my throat. I mourn all the times I laughed with pride for my superior ability to make things happen. I fall on my face at the feet of Jesus. He picks me up and kisses the top of my head. His kiss is the spark that reminds me I'm being re-created to be a new kind of citizen in a new kind of world. As I said, I'm learning to give careful thought to my ways, including the ways I work. The kiss of God is the currency of the new, free world. It's this currency I want more and more of.

Imagination and Creativity

Imagine with me, if you will: It is the sixties, sometime between JFK's assassination and the arrival of the hippies to San Francisco's Haight-Ashbury district. I'm just a child, one child among several seated in a classroom. There are four neat rows of desks with six desks to a row. Each desk, constructed of wood and steel, has an inkwell hole at the top. Since the universal conversion from ink to number-two pencils, the only activity the inkwell enjoys is the rush of gravity as a crumpled piece of paper or a wad of Bazooka bubblegum drops from the hand of a student into the cavity of the desk. For children, this confirms the pleasure of simple things.

I'm lucky. I have my pleasures, too. My desk is number four in the row next to the windows that look out onto Plumas Street—the main street of Yuba City, my hometown. From my coveted position I have a reasonably unobstructed view of the front door of the corner store where I will most certainly purchase cinnamon toothpicks when the last bell rings and I am set free.

Still I have my days, wistful days, when the autumn breeze dances through the open windows with such enticement and abandon that I cannot resist climbing aboard for a ride. Straddling the wind, I hold on for life and carefully navigate the slender gap between the open window and its sill. Wide open space. I rocket into the sky, then fall and dart like the swallow. High above the street I conclude there are more rich people in my little town than I'd thought. There are so many swimming pools.

When I tire of flight, I'm back in my seat, busy, shrinking. I make myself small enough to walk along the top of my teacher's desk. I climb onto the open pages of her grade book and look for my name. I don't find it; I hear it.

"Chuck, turn around in your seat and face the blackboard."

And with those words, I'm brought back to size. I've been caught imagining, again.

Have you ever been caught imagining?

Imagination is the power at work in us that allows us to dream of something within the mind, to see or hear it before it actually exists. When you think of the imagination, think of it as calling into the mind such things as communication, mathematics, physics, scenarios, images, or sounds. These and those like them start in the mind and remain in the mind. Did I really fly? Did I really shrink?

To imagine is to dive deep into an ocean of possibilities. What can the imagination see with eyes closed? What can it construct without moving a finger? What can it taste though the tongue is locked up tight? What can it hear? The answer is, innumerable things, infinite images, choices, and sounds, far more than we can describe or name. In truth, what the mind can imagine is so great that you or I could never think of or catalog it all in a lifetime. In a few minutes' time, one dreamer can imagine something that might take one hundred people a lifetime to create. This is the power of imagination.

The breadth, height, and depth of the imagination are never known in full by any one man or woman. It's too vast and, truthfully, too good to be known by us in such a way. The fullness of imagination is God's and God's alone. Nevertheless, each of us has an important role to play in contributing to the collective imagination of our time. Every contribution is significant to history.

Though an artist, I work hard at rescuing the imagination from the misconception that it applies to the arts or artists alone. It doesn't. It is a major component of the new way to be human. Without the ethical imagination, there is no healthy, God-glorifying, whole-life spirituality. The imagination is necessary to moral and ethical reflection and often inspires the actions that come out of such reflection. Imagination can be the purring and perfectly tuned engine of a truly good, creative life. Every student-follower of Jesus ought to be prayerfully and wisely using what C. S. Lewis called the "organ of meaning." The good imagination is good for people and planet. When we use it in ways congruent with the heart of God, we show the brilliance of his ways. Showing God's brilliance is a major component of the new way.

Over the years I've done some thinking on the role of the imagination in creating a life story founded on and informed by the Story, specifically the shape and brightness of biblical ethics. The link between imagination and ethics is an important one. No follower of Jesus should be without the clues, and I've been enthusiastically digging for them. When the imagination and biblical ethics come together to create good, the image of God in humankind shines bright, and shining bright is a goal of every student-follower.

At seminary I took a course from a wise and quirky professor named David Clyde Jones. Jones defines biblical ethics as "the study of the way of life that conforms to the will of God as revealed in Christ and the Holy Scriptures and illuminated by the Holy Spirit. It seeks to answer the practical question: What is God calling us, his redeemed people, to be and to do?"[1]

In terms of goals, persons, and practices, Jones gives a threefold answer to what God is calling us to be and do. He says, "The *controlling purpose* of the Christian life is the glory of God; the *impelling motive* of the Christian life is love for God; and the *directing principle* of the Christian life is the will of God as revealed in Christ and the Holy Scriptures"[2] (emphasis added).

Jones points out that the will of God—or the directing principle of the new way to be human—is clearly seen in Jesus's twofold commandment found in Matthew 22:37-40 and the threefold summary of the will of God found in Micah 6:8. These texts, taken together, focus the will of God for us and help define a simple, yet foundational biblical ethic:

1. Love the Lord your God with all your soul, heart, and mind.
2. Love your neighbor as yourself.
3. Act justly.
4. Love mercy and show kindness.
5. Walk humbly and faithfully with God.

For the sake of definition, when referring to ethics, this is the biblical foundation I'm building on.

A moment ago I introduced a starting place for thinking about imagination. Now I'll nuance it a bit.

In her book *The Disciplined Heart*, Caroline J. Simon argues that "love, according to the Christian story, gives insight into the true end toward which we aspire, which (humanly) does not yet appear."[3] She calls this form of insightful love *imagination*. I wholeheartedly agree and would want this to be another necessary part of a working explanation of *imagination*. I strongly believe that imagination is love that sees with wisdom and insight. It is "a way of seeing life."[4] It sees possibilities for expressing love and brings them forth out of the ocean of one's image-bearing capacity, then parades these possibilities before the mind's eye. If creativity is the drama, then imagination is the script. If life is the film, then imagination is the storyboard.

This isn't the forum to analyze the differing ways Aristotle, Kant, Hume, Sartre, or Rorty have sought to explain imagination (nor do I have the skill necessary). Instead, I'll play the artist card and offer my simple and personal interpretation.

I approach imagination epistemologically—as a God-given tool for a way of knowing that leads to ways of being and doing congruent with the will of God. In short, what I call the good imagination leads to an embodiment of God's ways that are God-loving, neighbor-loving, and God-glorifying. When I use the word *imagination,* this is the goal I have in mind.

I also allow for imagination to be both a clear mental representation of an idea (an image) and the mental faculty to *see* possibilities (without producing a true, exacting mental image).

I believe that all cognizant humans possess imagination and use it daily in various ways. I also maintain that all cognizant humans are creative and that they fill the earth with their creativity—good and evil, excellent and poor, useful and worthless. These abilities, active today, were imparted to the first humans at their creation, when God saw fit to make man and woman in his image. It is important for everyone everywhere to understand that imagination and creativity are not limited to people with artistic skill. On the contrary, to be human—alive and aware—is to possess the ability to imagine and create. I find no merit in the shaky argument that human creativity is romantic in origin rather than biblical.

Imagination is the soil out of which creativity grows. For example, with regard to music, if the role of the imagination is to imagine melody, then the role of creativity is to make it heard in everyday life. The imagination is responsible for musical dreams, while creativity is responsible for making musical dreams come to pass. One thinks, the other acts. One is a hidden word, the other is visible work. The imagination asks, "What if?" Creativity answers, "Here it is."

Imagination is not neutral though. The presence of sin in the human family ensures that the imagination can be sinful as well as good. For example, the good imagination helped Handel create the *Messiah,* but the imagination also helped King David see in his mind's eye what it would mean to possess the beautiful nakedness of Bathsheba. While Handel's imagination created beauty, joy, and worship, King David's imagination was the soil in which even more sin took root. And David's first sin led to at least two deaths. Such is the power of the imagination.

Immeasurable acts of creativity are born out of the simplest of imaginings. For centuries, children had imagined the ability to fly like a bird or to shrink themselves so small as to travel in places where the human body could not go. Now, in our time, we do fly—in rockets, jets, and gliders, and through laparoscopic surgery we shrink small enough to travel inside the human body. How did this come to be? Someone went beyond imagining to the tangible creation of these extraordinary inventions. What they imagined, they created. And what once did not exist now exists. Imagination and creativity are a powerfully good pair and woefully misunderstood, especially by people professing to follow Jesus—which is a contradiction of some consequence.

Imagination and creativity are often confused with each other. While people use these words interchangeably, they do not share a common meaning. Each one is distinctive and important to ways of being human. For example, I might say of my son: "Sam is very creative." If I mean that Sam creates often, such as writing two or three songs a day, then my statement stands as accurate. However, if I mean to communicate that Sam has sharpened his ability to dream of the good possibilities for music, then I should say, "My son, Sam, is very imaginative."

It is important to hold imagination and creativity apart and not bind their individual meanings permanently together in the one word. Why? Returning to my illustration, it's possible for Sam to dream of the good possibilities for music without ever acting on them. Imagination does not have to be acted upon. When it is, though, creativity results. In short, you can imagine without creating, but you cannot truly create with intentionality without first imagining. Imagination is a first cause. It acts as a kind of buffer zone for what could be done in the immediate or distant future. In all intentional creativity, a first cause is born in the imagination of someone somewhere sometime. This can be made even clearer through another illustration.

If I go to a crafts store and purchase a kit to paint a waterfall scene and follow the directions exactly—that is, I stay within the prescribed lines, use color number nine for section six, and so on—by my definition I'm being creative. I'm making something new that wasn't in the world before I chose to bring it into the world. However, my ability to imagine was never put to use in the creation of the painting, was it? Instead, the imagination of an unknown artist or marketer was the first cause of the waterfall painting. Someone was paid to come up with the outline that I filled in. This illustrates why I say that in all intentional creativity, there is a first cause born in the imagination of someone somewhere sometime. There is still more to glean from this illustration.

My waterfall painting should not be construed as evidence for anything other than my ability to create. It doesn't make me very creative or very imaginative or as I've already pointed out, even imaginative at all. It is simply evidence that I can create. In short: I am human, therefore I create.

Also, just because I imagine and create doesn't mean that I do so in ways that show a real depth of possibility, which would be very imaginative. Likewise, just because I imagine and create doesn't mean I make a lot of things, which would be very creative. Finally, just because I use my imagination and create something doesn't mean that what I've dreamed up or created is aesthetically or morally good. This brings us to the issue of quality.

When a person is said to be creative, it is assumed that what he or she creates is above average in quality, as illustrated by the sentence: "Jenny is creative; ask her to come up with an idea for the Rose Parade float." What is conveyed through this sentence is the norm in society. If someone is said to be creative, or very creative, it usually means that whatever he or she does creatively is well above average, even excellent. I don't expect my thoughts on the subject to change a common manner of speaking (even if it is inaccurate). What's most important is to see that misusage and misunderstanding help to keep the connection between imagination, creativity, and biblical ethics permanently severed. Whenever our ways of speaking serve the goal of keeping imagination and creativity out of the business of following Jesus, there's a problem.

Both imagination and creativity can be accounted for and judged in terms of quantity and quality. If I describe the link between quantity, imagination, and creativity in the most basic terms, it's the presence of some amount of ideas leading to some amount of stuff. The link between quality, imagination, and creativity is just as simple. The quantity of ideas and stuff is under judgment morally, ethically, and aesthetically. In many instances, the norms of popular culture arbitrate quality. Since popular culture has many niches and distinct communities, there are many opinions about what is or isn't quality. These opinions may or may not have anything to do with historical views of morality, ethics, or aesthetics.

My thought is that quality, in the here and now, should be measured by a comprehensive standard, one big enough for the whole of life. Which brings me back to David Clyde Jones and his controlling purpose, impelling motive, and directing principle. The controlling purpose is God's excellence, his glory. This is the front where human rebellion fights strongest. Many say that God is not, that he doesn't exist. Others say that God is not excellent. What Jones is saying is that the purpose of life is to declare that God is in fact excellent in every way. The controlling Story introduced in chapters 1 and 2 of Genesis is nothing less than a declaration of God's preeminent excellence. The Fall did nothing to alter God's excellence, only that of his creation.

From this start, Jones takes us to Matthew 22:37-40 and Micah 6:8. These passages form a biblical ethic built to last. They give people a foundation for being and doing, within which imaginings and creative output fit squarely. How does what I imagine and desire to create reflect love for God and neighbor? How will it show God's excellence? How does it reflect faithfulness to God's agenda in the world? Is it merciful, kind, and just?

Because God's ways of being human do include standards, we can't speak of the quality of imagination and creativity without using words that describe the fulfillment of the standard (excellence), its wanton violation (evil), and all points in between. This also gets more complex as you consider that quality has an ethical and aesthetic side to it. We adjust our words to fit the circumstance when analyzing the ethical and aesthetic side of imagination and creativity.

The way to really get inside this is to return to the words *creational* and *relational*. In the Story of God-people-and-place, there exists Creational Norms and Relational Norms. God, as Artist and Storyteller, is the first cause of both. If we want to know Creational Norms, we watch him work. If we want to know Relational Norms, we listen to him speak. Because of Jesus and the new way, we have the clearest picture ever of Creational and Relational Norms or ways to live. True quality is composed of these two sides: the ethical and the aesthetic. The first, the ethical, is related to God's relational Word, his will for his people. The second, the aesthetic, is related to God's creational Word, the vast array of all that God has made. This is where I find the most complete direction for imagining and creating.

The ability to image God should never be overlooked. It serves as the foundation for human existence with four cornerstone-like aspects on which all our being and doing on earth are constructed. These are: (1) the ability to imagine and think; (2) the ability to create; (3) the ability to make moral and ethical choices and act on them (to be holy); and (4) the ability to act freely, to choose what kinds of persons we will become. In all these ways human beings are like God—and yet we are his creation and clearly not God.

Not only are our imagination and creativity products of our image-bearing ability, but so is our ability to assess them. God has given us the responsibility to govern the earth and its inhabitants. Part of this governing role is to make judgments about the quality of creativity we bring into the world. Nevertheless, our human responsibility does not render God mute. He has made his will known, having spoken via his creative Word (creation) and his relational Word (self-disclosure). In short, sufficient knowledge of the will of God has been made known to the human family so that we are without excuse. The human family, created to create and govern, has not been left without instructions for ways of thinking, imagining, and doing that are pleasing to God. God's ways are the collective, controlling Story for all our storytelling and storied living. God's ways are the standard.

Yet human beings, because of their sinful nature, are bent on rebellion—on choosing contrary to God's ways. This pervasive sinfulness and damage are what cause our imaginations and creativity to move in the opposite direction of God's ways. It's the reason that the quality of our imagining and creating is often something other than the good God would have us be and do.

~

I've been using art-related illustrations as an accommodation to the way most people look at imagination and creativity. It's time to see how imagination and creativity are linked to the new way to be human in general.

Imagine that I'm driving east on Interstate 40 outside of Nashville, Tennessee. A quarter of a mile ahead of me, on my side of the road, is a car parked along the shoulder with its hood up. As I get closer, I see a young woman leaning against the car. I become concerned for her and begin to imagine myself pulling over to ask if she needs assistance. In a micromeasure of time, I imagine slowing down, parking in front of her, and talking to her from a distance so as not to frighten her. I imagine the consequences of my choice. I may need to call Andi to let her know I'll be late for our lunch meeting. I may need to give this person a lift or let her use my cell phone. She may be scared and very uncomfortable having to talk to a strange man alone on the side of the freeway. I think to myself: *Remember this, be of help and put her at ease with your choice of words and body language. Treat her the way you'd want a stranger to treat Andi if she were stalled along the road.* Good, got it.

Zoom! I drive right past her. I don't stop.

The work of my imagination was wasted. I failed to stop and do the creative, caring work I'd imagined doing. My imagination had no immediate effect on earth because it was not acted upon. I drive on to my lunch meeting with Andi.

Now here's a second scenario. Imagine that a mile behind me is Jim in a black Isuzu Trooper. He's coming up on the same scene I just passed at seventy miles an hour. He imagines himself pulling over to ask if the woman needs assistance. In a micromeasure of time, he imagines slowing down, parking in front of her, and talking to her from a distance so as not to frighten her. When it looks as if she's no longer alarmed, he will come a little closer, and then a little closer. Jim imagines the consequences of his choice. He'll need to call his wife to let her know he plans to work late into the evening. The woman seems very relaxed now, maybe even interested in something beyond getting her car started. He'll stay calm and cool, help her get her car going, and then see if he can buy her a drink.

Zoom! Jim drives right past her. He doesn't stop.

While my refusal to stop kept good from entering the world, Jim's refusal to stop kept evil intent from taking shape in the world (with regard to what Jim was responsible for). The harm—that is the self-serving sexual interest Jim imagined—had no effect on earth because it was not acted upon. He drove on to the office, felt like a fool for imagining such a scenario, worked the rest of the day, and returned home to his wife, grateful for not having acted on what he'd imagined.

There are, of course, two more related scenarios: (1) a person sharing my imaginings actually does stop to offer legitimate, caring help to the stranded motorist; and (2) a person sharing Jim's imaginings actually does stop, offers illegitimate self-serving help, and brings harm to the stranded motorist.

In all four scenarios the focus of the imagination is the same: the stranded motorist. When I focused on the motorist, I became concerned for her and immediately imagined helping. I imagined myself loving her with neighbor love, living out the summation of biblical ethics. But something happened; something went wrong. It seemed like too much trouble. I didn't want to be late for my meeting downtown. Certainly someone less busy would stop to help and everything would work out fine. I created an excuse, a rationalization to dismiss my imaginings.

It should be evident that there are instances when the imagination works, and yet creativity should be avoided. But the opposite is true as well. The imagination works, but creativity isn't pursued—and that is wrong. When this happens, good fails to make its way into the world. An opportunity to fulfill one's image-bearing role has been forfeited.

How do you know when imagination is good, when it ought to manifest itself in good and creative works? Ethically speaking, imagination is good when it reflects the ways of God for his people—his relational Word.

$\sim$

I trust the link between biblical ethics and the ability to imagine has been brought together with sufficient clarity. From this point forward I'll refer to their partnership as the ethical imagination.

I have made the point that imagination and creativity are God's equipping of the human family in order that we might image him. God created people to be like him in particular ways so that they would be equipped to love and work in ways of being and doing that mirror his. Our work is to create out of the creativity of God, to draw out its endless possibilities. The Creator made us to be little creators with the responsibility of meaningful work and purpose in the world. In review, all of this is revealed to us in the very first chapters of Genesis (see Genesis 1:26–2:25).

Because sin and death entered the human story at the Fall, humans can no longer mirror God faithfully or perfectly. Yet as flawed as they may be, humans still have the ability to image God. The presence of this ability as an essential part of a biblical anthropology is not in dispute. Keeping this firmly in mind, let's look at the biblical narrative for evidence of imagination.

In Genesis 6:5 we read that "God saw that the wickedness of man was great in the earth and that *every imagination of the thoughts of his heart* was only evil continually" (KJV, emphasis added).

In the book of Nehemiah we see evidence of someone who imagines problems that don't exist: "Nothing like what you are saying is happening; you are just making it up out of your head" (6:8).

The Bible speaks of people who "plot deception" (Psalm 38:12), "a heart that devises wicked schemes" (Proverbs 6:18), and those who "imagine mischief" (Psalm 62:3, KJV).

The book of Ezekiel has some harsh words for foolish prophets: "Son of man, prophesy against the prophets of Israel who are now prophesying. Say to those who prophesy out of their own imagination: 'Hear the word of the LORD! This is what the Sovereign LORD says: Woe to the foolish prophets who follow their own spirit and have seen nothing!'" (13:2-3).

Jesus connects imagination with lust in Matthew 5:28: "But I tell you that anyone who looks at a woman lustfully has already committed adultery with her in his heart."

The Bible clearly reveals the function of the imagination in sinful behavior. It shows it being used illegitimately. Nevertheless, the ability to imagine and create (to mirror God) should never be thought of as evil or sinful. Instead, we should live in acknowledgment that these powerful abilities are being renewed and restored for the purposes of God, through the redemption he's implemented in and through Messiah Jesus.

Patrick Henry, in his book *The Ironic Christian's Companion,* wrote that "the freeplay of imagination tells us more about God than do rules and precepts."[5] This is quite different from what I've been saying. In my view, it is the kingdom rule of God—his ways—that directs the function and fruit of the imagination. God certainly uses the "freeplay of imagination" in helping us understand him and our role in his universe, but our imaginings never trump his Story. Instead, they're guided by his self-disclosure and serve it everywhere and in everything.

It is doubtful that painter Jacqueline Matute would agree with me. According to Matute, "Art allows me to use an unlimited imagination with colors and sexuality that bring attention to our subconscious in a visual manner." Unlike Matute, I would not argue for an unlimited imagination in art or otherwise. Neither would I advocate a stunted imagination. You certainly don't see such a thing in the norm God puts forth in his imaginative creation. What I'm saying is that there are clear human limitations to imagination in this world at this time. There is boundary and mystery. The ethical imagination by definition is a limited imagination that must leave room for mystery. It actually hopes to avoid dreaming of every possibility and acting on it toward a creative end. The ethical imagination is an imagination surrendered to Jesus's twofold commandment articulated in Matthew 22:37-40, the threefold summary of the will of God found in Micah 6:8, and the controlling purpose of God's excellence being known.

When viewed from a biblical position, the limiting of the imagination is a good thing. Yet focusing our sole attention on keeping the imagination within limits is not the point at all. To do so is to miss out on what it means to be human. How? There is also a way in which the imagination should know no limits, that is, in the imagining of good for the glory, the love, and the will of God. This is the vocation of all who follow Jesus in the new way to be human.

Faking and Forgetting

In Matthew 16:13-17, the story goes that "when Jesus came to the region of Caesarea Philippi, he asked his disciples, 'Who do people say the Son of Man is?'

"They replied, 'Some say John the Baptist; others say Elijah; and still others, Jeremiah or one of the prophets.'

"'But what about you?' he asked. 'Who do you say I am?'

"Simon Peter answered, 'You are the Christ, the Son of the living God.'

"Jesus replied, 'Blessed are you, Simon son of Jonah, for this was not revealed to you by man, but by my Father in heaven.'"

As the story unfolds, we watch Simon Peter stumble and fail, but we also see him come alive as a leader in telling the Story of God-people-and-place. When he answered Jesus honestly and accurately, he showed an understanding of God's relational and creational will. It was as if he was saying, "Jesus, you are the Word made flesh. You are a promise kept." Then as if to show how easily he could profess the profound and turn back to his old life, three times Peter denied even knowing Jesus.

The same way that we proclaim Jesus and his kingdom, we deny him—through our word and work. Real following, as Peter found out, costs you your life. It costs you your understanding of word and work. If you refuse to trade your understanding of word and work for God's, he lets you keep yours, and then you find out you've understood nothing and worked for nothing. One of the strange upside-down things about the life of following Jesus is that you really want it to cost your life. If it doesn't, you've yet to step into the Story with intentionality. That's dangerous. It's the danger of dishonesty, of saying, "Yes, you are Messiah," and then going about your life as if he isn't. This is the lesson Peter learned, the one that caused him to weep bitterly.

When Peter named Jesus as Messiah, he was telling Jesus, "Look, I know who you are. You are the Anointed One, the Son of God, David's true heir, the King who has come to rescue Israel from the control of pagan culture. Over and over you talk about the kingdom! You've come to vindicate us, to relieve our suffering, and to gather us together as a returned-from-exile people. And if the exile has ended, then our sins are forgiven!"

What Peter did not know—yet—was whether Messiah Jesus would defeat Israel's enemies first in a military battle or would rebuild the temple. Jewish stories held that Messiah would be about both of these. And he would, but not in the way Peter (or Israel) thought.

Peter was already a student-follower. He had left behind his life and work of fishing to follow Jesus. To name his Teacher in this way meant that he knew his own student role would be shaped by his Teacher's identity and mission. What would following be if it wasn't following wherever the Teacher led?

Peter had no idea that Jesus did not intend to lead a battle against Israel's enemies or rebuild the physical temple or be installed as King of an earthly kingdom. Peter had yet to understand that the kingdom Jesus came to announce was an invitation to follow him and his agenda for life. It was indeed a rescue mission, but one that would come in stages. It was the rescue of everything, beginning with the community of Israel. The rescue involved making everything everywhere right again, so that the heavens and earth would be made new, and people would live out the new way to be human that Jesus revealed to them. The goal of rescue is God and his people in his place living under his rule.

After what the story calls Pentecost, all genuine followers were and still are without excuse. Once Peter had no idea, and then he knew. From that point forward he gave up his life for the way, the truth, and the life—Jesus, the King. The King's business became his business, and there was no other life apart from it. This is still the way to be human today. It is the way to be single. It is the way to be married.

If we live differently than this while professing Messiah, then something is wrong, right? The King of Twists lures us into a kind of twistedness where dishonesty gets mistaken for maturity. This happens when a person or a married couple excels at faking and forgetting for so long that people actually think the person or couple is mature in Jesus (simply because they appear to have it together). When I say faking, I mean pretending that nothing's wrong and everything's fine. When I say forgetting, I mean living by some other agenda than God's. Forgetting is thinking that success, well-being, safety, and peace can be found in something or someone other than God. Student-followers of Jesus cannot afford to appear to have it all together by the world's standards. Better to be weak and following the way than to have your false glory be your shame.

Things would have to be really out of whack for this to become a lifestyle among the people of God, correct? Let me take you to an old book from the Story, Haggai 1:1-9:

> In the second year of King Darius, on the first day of the sixth month, the word of the LORD came through the prophet Haggai to Zerubbabel son of Shealtiel, governor of Judah, and to Joshua son of Jehozadak, the high priest:
> This is what the LORD Almighty says: "These people say, 'The time has not yet come for the LORD's house to be built.'"
> Then the word of the LORD came through the prophet Haggai: "Is it a time for you yourselves to be living in your paneled houses, while this house remains a ruin?"

Now this is what the LORD Almighty says: "Give careful thought to your ways. You have planted much, but have harvested little. You eat, but never have enough. You drink, but never have your fill. You put on clothes, but are not warm. You earn wages, only to put them in a purse with holes in it."

This is what the LORD Almighty says: "Give careful thought to your ways. Go up into the mountains and bring down timber and build the house, so that I may take pleasure in it and be honored," says the LORD. "You expected much, but see, it turned out to be little. What you brought home, I blew away. Why?" declares the LORD Almighty. "Because of my house, which remains a ruin, while each of you is busy with his own house."

Contextually, this is a story about temple building. In the larger Story of God-people-and-place, it also relates to the church, the gathering. The temple of the new way is the church. As God rebuilds a people for himself, he is most concerned with the spiritual, because it's a spiritual house he's building. Jesus is the foundation, and the church is the new Israel— a people of God made up of every race and ethnicity. It's a new nation without borders. This is why 1 Peter 2:4-5 says, "As you come to him, the living Stone—rejected by men but chosen by God and precious to him— you also, like living stones, are being built into a spiritual house to be a holy priesthood, offering spiritual sacrifices acceptable to God through Jesus Christ."

Your spiritual sacrifice is a sincere and contrite heart moving in the long and obedient direction of Jesus's kingdom agenda for life.

~⌐~

When we build lives or marriages of our own design, structure church of our own design, and allow some other story than God's to control life, we accept something short of the agenda of God. Of course, we start with

Jesus as the foundation, but we quickly shift to a different, more familiar architectural plan: us. When we do, faking and forgetting are at the doorstep. Because we've started with God, our sin easily seduces us into thinking that everything we build after the Jesus foundation is of God as well. But often it's not. We build our own house, not God's. If we end up with human structure and no vital house of God in the world, no salty salt or bright light of the church, we will have failed our mission.

Even though there is always something wrong with the people of God, we should never get comfortable with the idea. We should never say, "What's the use? Sin will always be with us." Just because problems are real and recurrent doesn't mean we should stop critiquing ourselves and asking for more grace. Neither should we lose hope that each morning is a new opportunity to follow more faithfully in the ways of Jesus. Fatalism and forfeiture are not on the menu.

For all who have an interest, the first stage of work is honesty. We can't afford to be dishonest about our condition. To be humble and contrite before God is to be honest before him. Faking and forgetting is not an option. Questions of truth and authenticity, what is real and what is fake, are not the primary domain of the idealist young. They are not something you once had, then became wise and mature and so let go of. These are the concerns of all who call themselves followers of Jesus, regardless of age or years in the community of faith.

It's a fact that people lose authenticity and begin faking and forgetting when other controlling stories shape them more than the Story of Jesus. Peter Berger says that a life of faking and forgetting is "more or less a comfortable settling down with the half-truths" and "the organized delusions which are embodied in the various social institutions"[1]—what I've already referred to as socially agreed-upon contexts.

This is how dishonesty can be mistaken for maturity. When we settle down with half-truths and organized delusions, we forget to build God's house and to be his people. We busy ourselves *with ourselves* and put off building a people for the purpose and pleasure of God. Calmly and coolly, many of us go about making a beautiful so-called Christian life where blessing and the American dream are synonymous. We become seduced by stories that promise freedom and then enslave us. "Busy, busy, busy— and for what?" the prophet asks. So we can trade the gift of God for a life with holes in it? "Give careful thought to your ways," God says, "give careful thought to your ways."

If you're like me, you're haunted by the feeling that something is very wrong with God's house. You know something, and so do I. Guess what? The only way to make it go away is to do something about it, or cover it over with faking and forgetting. I ask myself, What am I prepared to do? This brings to mind a conversation between Morpheus and Neo in the film *The Matrix*.

Morpheus: "Let me tell you why you're here. You're here because you know something. What you know, you can't explain, but you feel it. You've felt it your entire life—that there's something wrong with the world. You don't know what it is, but it's there like a splinter in your mind driving you mad. It is this feeling that has brought you to me. Do you know what I'm talking about?"

Neo: "The Matrix?"

Morpheus: "Do you want to know what it is? The Matrix is everywhere. It is all around us. Even now in this very room. You can see it when you look out your window or when you turn on your television. You can feel it when you go to work, when you go to church, when you pay your taxes. It is the world that has been pulled over your eyes to blind you from the truth."

Neo: "What truth?"

Morpheus: "That you are a slave, Neo. Like everyone else you were born into bondage, born into a prison that you cannot smell or taste or touch—a prison for your mind. Unfortunately, no one can be told what the Matrix is—you have to see it for yourself. As long as the Matrix exists, the human race will never be free."[2]

Something invisible enslaves the people of God. You can call it worldliness, sin, or the Matrix. Whatever name you give it, you have to see it for yourself. This is the first step toward the kind of freedom that allows individuals and couples to be the Art of God in the world. It's okay that it's like a splinter in our minds, that it's driving us mad and we can't fake the fact that it's there. This is good. It's putting an end to the faking and forgetting.

As we read in Haggai, people are always saying (through word and work) that the time is not right for them to move or to act more faithfully. Nothing is different in our time. It's not that people don't believe that good should be done. They do. The problem is that there is never a right time for it. Our excuses reveal that our priorities are elsewhere. We are all faithful to something though, aren't we? Our own personal lives and circumstances capture our attention far more than the agenda of God in this world. Jesus knows this. Into a world that lives by the mantra *"The time has not yet come,"* Jesus comes announcing that *the time has come* and that *the kingdom of God is near.* This message stands as is for everyone in every generation. Now is the time to give careful thought to our ways. We can't afford to become indifferent, to forfeit our integrity, to become fakers and forgetters, coasting through life as if our ways define it. The worst thing that could possibly happen is for us to get our way.

～

Followers of Jesus tell the world through word and work that we've come to believe there is one Story, one way of viewing God, humanity, nature, earth, and sky that makes the meaning of life more clear than all others. We believe it to be the Story of everyone everywhere at all times. In other words, not private religion, but public reality. Such a story leaves little

room for indifference, apathy, faking, forgetting, or dreaming uniquely
American dreams.

Douglas Coupland, in his book *Life After God,* wrote:

> Sometimes I think the people to feel the saddest for are people
> who are unable to connect with the profound—people such as my
> boring brother-in-law, a hearty type so concerned with normality
> and fitting in that he eliminates any possibility of uniqueness for
> himself and his own personality. I wonder if some day, when he is
> older, he will wake up and the deeper part of him will realize that
> he has never allowed himself to truly exist, and he will cry with
> regret and shame and grief.
>
> And then sometimes I think the people to feel saddest for are
> people who once knew what profoundness was, but who lost or
> became numb to the sensation of wonder—people who closed the
> doors that lead us into the secret world—or who had the doors
> closed for them by time and neglect and decisions made in times
> of weakness.[3]

The message couldn't be clearer. Give careful thought to your ways.
Don't trade the profound for a life of regret and shame. Don't let the organized delusions of the world close the doors that lead to a new and better
world. My friend Doug McKelvey wrote an insightful lyric that arrests me
every time I sing it:

> Oh it always amazed me
> How someone could come
> To the edge of the world
> Drop a stone down the side
> And turn and return to the very same life.[4]

One of the things I really love about some of my non-Christian artist friends is that they're not as obsessed with the culture's organized delusions, its understanding of normality and fitting in. They don't (in most cases) limit the possibilities in life, and they are far from numb to the sensation of wonder. In these ways they inspire me. And often they graciously allow me to speak frankly about what I believe the spiritual life to be. I'm thankful for their openness. They don't fear the dialogue. They fear being deceived or duped. They fear being sold a story that isn't authentic, isn't worth bothering with. Sometimes they protect themselves against this by believing nothing at all—or by believing everything. In any case, they seem to instinctively know that something as serious as one's relationship to God, the human family, and to earth and sky ought to be handled with care and a degree of seriousness and commitment. The question for those who already follow is obvious.

The Kingdom Way

Giving careful thought to our ways means learning to bring the new Jesus agenda to bear upon all of life. This is an activity that involves a continual Spirit-inspired renewal of the mind, and intentional, faithful word and work on our part. In practice this means picking any area of human activity and working to understand how it fits within the new way and what it means to cooperate with Jesus's agenda.

Let's use education as an example. The first thing to do is to come to terms with what I understand education to be. Is education only a means to an end, a job? Is it something I have to do but wouldn't do if it didn't seem to be my only option? Or is it part of what it means to be human? The latter, I think. Its connection goes right back to Genesis. To answer the call to care for God's Word and work is to enter into a life of learning where everything God has spoken and created is both the basis of education and the need for education. For instance, how can we care for the oceans of the world if we don't understand them?

Long ago, people took the first steps of educating themselves about the sea. They shared this knowledge with others, and those people built new knowledge on top of the foundation. It's been this way throughout the ages. This is what we do with respect to everything under the sun (actually, including the sun). All of us are learners and educators in some form. We are being educated in something every moment of the day, and of course, we're learning too. For followers of Jesus "education is not about getting more information. It is about transformation."[1] Education ought to be about cooperating with God's agenda to transform our ways of being human. Education can teach me theology and oceanography, and both of these (when good) can help transform me into a better caretaker of God's Word and work (such as the oceans of the world).

Education affects how well we cooperate with God's agenda. It's not as simple as excelling in school, getting a college degree, entering into well-paid work, and calling it a day. Professing Christians should stop perpetuating this myth. Real education is communally constructed, often out of several communities—intersecting or not—across a lifetime. It's didactic *and* liquid, seen and unseen. Most important, good education helps people want to be good and, as a result, do good. "I want to be a direct representative of God in this world" can and should lead to all sorts of activity, including "I want to do good music."

Do schools, colleges, and universities help in accomplishing this? Of course. What concerns me, though, is how the Community of Invitation works together to see that people are prepared for "works of service" in the most comprehensive way possible, over a lifetime.

In my world I steward many things—among them influence, knowledge, goods, services, and money. Influence is a by-product of my story. I don't control it or spend any time worrying about whether I have it or not. I'm aware that I possess some influence only because my community says I do. Knowledge is also a by-product of my story. The goal is to possess transforming knowledge or wisdom. My goods and services are things like the Art House, books and CDs, a recording studio, and skill and ability in writing, teaching, and music. I'm a worker in the world, and money is the primary means of exchange in the marketplace. Like influence and knowledge, goods, services, and money are by-products of my unfolding story too. These are on loan from God for his purposes in the world.

If I'm really serious about seeing that God's people are educated and equipped, I'll pray, watch, and listen for when and where I can give to others the time and resources God has given me. But I can only be spontaneous in this to the degree that I haven't exhausted my time and resources. Simply put, it's like this: *Jesus, I have a general idea of what I'm doing with 75 percent of the time and resources you've entrusted to me, and I'm eagerly waiting to see what opportunities you create for the other 25 percent.*

Let's imagine together for a moment. I go about my usual Art House work and through it meet a couple with a very musically talented child. They don't have the knowledge or the resources to fan the flame of this child's gifts, but I do. I have musical expertise, instruments and recording equipment, and the ability to gift financially. Should I get involved in the education of their child? What business is it of mine? Actually, for direct representatives of God in the world, this is kingdom business. I've been entrusted with caring for God's creativity and making the new way to be human known. The child's parents may in the end decline any help, but this shouldn't keep me from asking, "Father, I'd like to serve this family and child. Do you want me to reveal your generosity to them now or later?" I ask with confidence because I already know that the Story reminds me "to do good, to be rich in good deeds, and to be generous and willing to share" (1 Timothy 6:18). I know that by following Jesus I've been made rich in every way so that I can be generous on every occasion, and through my generosity people will thank God (2 Corinthians 9:11). I'm not in any way suggesting that people become a series of projects though. In kingdom work we make our requests known in conversation with God, we seek discernment, and we move in faith. Timing, purpose, God's intentions, and the willingness of people to receive generosity all factor in.

In writing about this very subject, Dallas Willard looked to Bonhoeffer's book *Life Together* for inspiration. Willard summarized it this way: "Among those who live as Jesus' apprentices there are no relationships that omit the presence and action of Jesus. We never go 'one on one'; all relationships are mediated through him. I never think simply of what I am going to do with you, to you, or for you, I think of what we, Jesus and I, are going to do with you, to you, and for you."[2]

~~

From start to finish, here's a systematic look at how to make this portion of the kingdom way visible in the world:

1. Align yourself with the kingdom agenda by seeking good answers to questions like these: Why am I doing what I'm doing, and what does it have to do with God's agenda in the world? How am I making the kingdom rule visible? Does what I'm doing or thinking of doing have anything to do with the new way that Jesus modeled? Am I still interested in the same things Jesus is interested in?

2. Build into your life unscheduled time and uncommitted resources.

3. As his direct representative, ask yourself, What has God left me in charge of? What has God entrusted to me that I could share with others? Take an inventory of your resources and clearly understand what God has put you in charge of. Write it down. Everything counts. Don't rule out anything. You've read my general inventory, but here's another example:

   Tim, student, University of California, San Diego:
   - influence within the surf community, particularly surf clothing vendors
   - fluent in Spanish, with travel experience in South America
   - extremely fit
   - knowledgeable in Southern California plant life and soil conditions from two summers of working for Constantine Garden Supply
   - excellent writer

- has three extra surfboards not currently in use and boxes of clothing given to him by surf companies
- enjoys talking to senior citizens
- break dancer
- has $327.45 in his checking account

Where is your influence? What are you knowledgeable about? What goods, services, and money have you been entrusted with? At any point in the course of life, we need to know what God has left us in charge of.

4. Pick a subject, any subject, such as family, theology, neighbors or coworkers, prayer, horticulture, and so on. How would you define your subject? What do you understand it to be or mean? What, if anything, does the biblical story instruct regarding it? What are your resources for gaining further understanding, knowledge, and, ultimately, wisdom?

   Let's say you picked "neighbors." And let's imagine that you have a broad view of who your neighbor is. In other words, your neighbor is your roommate *and* a stranger halfway around the world. Hold on to this idea.

5. Regarding your subject—a person, the creation, an activity— pray, watch, and listen for when and where you can give the time and resources God has given to you. Talk to God about these important matters of mutual concern. In some way you are rich. Prepare your heart to be generous.

The new way to be human involves this kind of intentional being, knowing, thinking, imagining, and doing. Again, it's the word and work model of Jesus. Ask him, "Where is beauty needed? Where is restoration of the land needed? Where is renewal of a talent or gift needed? Where is a simple and quiet word needed? Where is the announcement of the good news, kingdom story needed?"

The work of a student-follower of Jesus is to push back the effects of the Fall, restore health whenever and wherever possible, encourage people to be fully human, holy, imaginative, and creative, and actually do what Jesus commanded his followers to do. If student-followers of Jesus took this way of living seriously, imagine the richness, meaning, and purpose each hour, day, month, and year would hold.

~——

At 4 p.m. on May 27, 1992, in the war-torn city of Sarajevo, people hungry for bread lined up outside a bakery. Without warning, a bomb fell and split the line into pieces, killing twenty-two people. Not far from the scene lived a musician named Vedran Smailovic. Before the weight of war crushed Sarajevo's music, Smailovic had been the principal cellist with the opera. At his wit's end and sickened by the slaughter, Smailovic made a choice that day. He decided to breathe life into the rubble of war.

> Every day thereafter, at 4 p.m., precisely, Vedran Smailovic put on his full, formal concert attire, took up his cello, and walked out of his apartment into the midst of the battle raging around him. He placed a little camp stool in the middle of the crater that the shell had made, and he played a concert. He played to the abandoned streets, to the smashed trucks and burning buildings, and to the terrified people who hid in the cellars while the bombs dropped and the bullets flew. Day after day, he made his unimaginably courageous stand for human dignity, for all those lost to war, for civilization, for compassion, and for peace.[3]

This is a picture of what the new way might look like in the wild world in which we live. Through this one daily act, Smailovic illustrated the calling to do good to all people and Jesus's command to "Love your enemies, do good to those who hate you" (Luke 6:27).

I have no idea whether Smailovic professed to follow Jesus. Nevertheless, there's something to be learned through his storied living. He preached through gut, wood, horsehair, and hands: "People of Sarajevo! People of Bosnia! We are made for so much more than this! Listen, we are made for beauty! Listen, we are made for truth! Listen, we are made for peace! Listen, be renewed, inspired, and cared for."

In the way he knew best, using the resources and talent before him, Smailovic exercised dominion over the crater in his neighborhood and pushed back the effects of the Fall. This was no neutral choice. It affected everyone around him, and its influence spread throughout the world. It was good storytelling and storied living. Two years later, on the stage of the Royal Conservatory Concert Hall in Manchester, England, the great Yo-Yo Ma performed David Wilde's composition "The Cellist of Sarajevo." Vedran Smailovic was there to hear it.

This kind of story should be the norm for followers of Jesus. I should rise each day and ask God, "What rubble do you want me to breathe your life into today? Where do you want the kingdom rule to be made visible? How can I help to make something or someone beautiful?" This kind of lifestyle is life-changing, and you never know how far or how long a story will travel on its trajectory of good.

I have a friend who tried for years to reconcile with her father. The woman had been abused as a child, and hatred for her father boiled under the surface of every word and action toward him. As an adult she received counseling and made several courageous efforts to confront him. No admission of guilt ever came. For twenty years she talked to Jesus about it, praying that she would be able to forgive and that her father would confess and repent. The hate turned to utter indifference, and the man became as good as dead to her. Then, surprisingly, one day he called and asked if he could visit.

Together with her husband, she fed her father a beautiful meal and they talked for an hour or so afterward, mostly about years long gone. He began his good-nights and good-byes, but the daughter wouldn't let him leave.

It wasn't easy, and it certainly wasn't perfect, but for the first time in her life the woman heard her father admit to what he had done. He asked her forgiveness and expressed hope that God would forgive him. She assured him that God's forgiveness was a conversation away. Then she and her husband told her father the Story of God-people-and-place and how sin had polluted human life. They told him, "Jesus is your hope of being made right again and free from thoughts and actions so contrary to what it means to be human. Following and trusting Jesus is the way of sin forgiveness. Don't bother trying to be good enough. He's the perfect good you can't yet be. Salvation is a gift from God to anyone who says, 'Thank you, Jesus. Looks like love to me.'" Then they closed their eyes and thanked God for doing for them what they couldn't do for themselves: heal the scars of unwellness. Peace came and it was a new day.

In the new way of Jesus, followers don't fake it. They clearly know something is wrong. They're perpetrators and they've been perpetrated against. But they also know how Jesus taught them to pray: "Forgive us our sins, for we also forgive everyone who sins against us." We forgive and we comfort with the comfort given us. This is the kingdom way and the new opportunity for life.

In the story I've just told, confession and forgiveness took the long way home—over thirty years to arrive. Sometimes good stories and good storied living take a long time to come to fruition. The Art of God is about quality, not expediency.

An interviewer once asked the famous rock keyboardist Rick Wakeman if he had talked to his close friend Ozzy Osbourne about the Christian faith. Rick responded, "Ozzy and I have discussed many things in the 30 years we've known each other and that has included God.... I'm not going to say any more on this subject as the things we discussed were pretty personal. Whilst my faith is well-known and I am always happy to discuss it openly whenever asked, I don't think it's right to talk about where another person is on their personal spiritual path, for in many cases only God is aware of it."[4]

We can be assured that the Artist is aware and at work in all things and is no slave to time as we understand it.

I attended a lecture at Vanderbilt University by Archbishop Emeritus Desmond Tutu. He made the comment that human relations depend on our memory. As the head of South Africa's Truth and Reconciliation Commission, Archbishop Tutu knows the importance of storytelling for the healing of a person, a community, and a country. The truth-telling aspect of story has a spiritual and therapeutic power. The TRC was set up by the government to help deal with what happened under apartheid. Three committees work to identify human rights violations, restore victim's dignity, and help with the rehabilitation and healing of survivors, their families and communities—and to allow applicants to apply for amnesty for any act, omission, or offense associated with a political objective during apartheid. Amnesty is granted only to those who will come forward, remember their story, and tell it to the committee—and victims or relatives of victims whenever possible. Once a perpetrator publicly remembers the story in the sight of his or her victims, there is the hope and real possibility of his or her reintegration into the community. Because stories get told, healing can begin. This is restorative rather than retributive justice. Though it's not always possible because of the stone coldness of the human heart, it is nevertheless always desirable.

In the story of the woman and her father, her greatest block to true forgiveness wasn't a need for more theological knowledge, but the very real need to have her story acknowledged and remembered. Zora Neale Hurston said it best in *Dust Tracks on a Road*: "There is no agony like bearing an untold story inside you."[5]

A similar setup to the TRC exists for followers of Jesus. James, the brother of Jesus wrote, "Therefore confess your sins to each other and pray for each other so that you may be healed. The prayer of a righteous man is powerful and effective" (James 5:16). So it is that people come forward, remember their story, tell it to Jesus, receive forgiveness and reconciliation, exchange their life plan for his, and then turn and follow him in the new way. Then whenever sin knocks them off course, they confess their sins to each other and pray for each other. They remember their sins and the One who takes away the sin of the world, Jesus. And peace comes again.

Man and woman are made to image God with holiness and creativity. Now, through Jesus, God is fulfilling his promise to renew the image within so that people become like his Son in word and work. Followers of Jesus are called to a life of making the new way to be human visible in the world for all to see. It's word and flesh, dreaming and doing.

The idea of caring for everything everywhere with holiness and imagination is at the heart of word and work in the new way. In friendship, marriage, family, education, and all human enterprise from homemaking to music making, the questions we ask of ourselves, of our thoughts, speech, and work are critical. Why am I doing what I'm doing, and what does it have to do with God's agenda in the world? How am I making the kingdom rule visible? What does this have to do with the new way to be human that Jesus modeled for his people? Am I still interested in the same things Jesus is interested in? When I forget to ask these questions, problems begin to surface. When things go really wrong, I find myself using 100 percent of my time and resources doing something I can't connect to God's kingdom agenda.

Years ago Andi showed me something about the economy of time. She said to me, "You're so overcommitted you can't afford either a crisis or the gift of an unexpected, good opportunity." She was right. Once I understood this, I built into my schedule unscheduled time. Today I can deal with things that naturally go wrong. And I can be present and active in new opportunities or spontaneous meetings as God brings them to my attention. I apply this same principle to resources such as influence, goods, services, and money. If I expend all of these to their maximum, I have nothing left for surprises, good or bad.

Obedience to the Word is the engine of life. It was in the beginning, and it is today. It's about following, listening, and obeying the certain Word, Jesus. According to Dallas Willard, more than anything, "the practical irrelevance of actual obedience to Christ accounts for the weakened effect of Christianity in the world today."[6] He writes that "we just don't do what he said. We don't seriously attempt it. And apparently we don't know how to do it."[7]

As I've noted in earlier chapters, we were never made to do it alone. We have an empathetic hero in Jesus. He's run the race and will carry us to the finish line if necessary. Confident of this, in faith we should learn what Jesus said, and then attempt to do it. As far as how to do it, I'll pass on to you what I've seen in Jesus, the Story, and the lives of those who follow him. That's the best any of us can do.

⌁

Some time ago in my own study, I put together what I believe are ten essential "first things" in the new way. I hold on to these pretty tightly. They're my foundation, my starting place. When I get lost in a fog of unbelief, I preach them to myself. I offer them for your consideration:

1. There is only one Creator-God, and not many gods. This God, the one God, is a Tri-personal being: Father, Son, and Holy Spirit. He created living beings, man and woman, to be his direct representatives on earth. His controlling Story is God-people-and-place, as defined by his relational Word.

2. Don't throw away your confidence, your hope, your belief, in the veracity of the Son, Jesus, and his teaching. Be sure of the certain Word, Jesus. No matter how far you are in time from the first-century gathering, you are still a recipient of eyewitness testimony. It was passed on to you by the people of long memory. Now you keep it and pass it on too. Hang tight with the story that Jesus is indeed the embodiment of God coming to the rescue of that which he loves. He is the Jesus of history, Messiah, the Atonement, the Resurrection, the Life. His rescue is a gift, a grace, and not something to be earned. Learn what these historical facts mean, and let them shape you and your world.

3. *Christianity, or the ongoing gathering of Messiah people (or whatever you want to call what Jesus came inviting people to), was never about religion.* And it wasn't about starting a new religion as a substitute for Judaism. What Jesus offered then and now is a new opportunity for life—a new way to be human—one inescapably connected to himself, his life, death, resurrection, and the future re-creation of everything. This is what you hold out in word and work as an invitation to community.

4. *The new way to be human begins with faith and repentance.* These, along with love, define the new way throughout. Faith and repentance are the only good responses to hearing the good news of God's rescue initiative. God tells a person: "This is what I have planned. This is what I will accomplish." The man or woman replies: "Good plan, I believe you. I repent of my own plan. I was headed in the wrong direction. By faith, I'll walk with you instead."

5. *Be passionate about the Story.* Remember, you can't be passionate about something you don't know. Step into the Story with intentionality and intensity. Live as a passionate person, alive to God's ways. If not, why not? Ask yourself, What's squelching my passion? What is stealing or polluting my interest? Being passionate doesn't mean clichéd. If you need models for passion and intentionality (and everybody does), look beyond the clichéd behavior that passes for spiritual enthusiasm most of the time.

6. *Character and lifestyle changes have always come with following Jesus.* The very first step of the first follower was life altering. Following Jesus

still is, and the Spirit on earth in you ensures it. Cooperate with the Spirit. There's freedom in following, freedom from all forms of enslavement and addiction (those that come from within and from without). Followers walk the road of reconciliation in the world with God and one another. God is reconciling people and place toward a good future.

7. *Involve yourself in diverse community whenever it's in your power to do so.* Better yet, seek it out and sponsor it. Eschew status. All people are welcome in the kingdom. Make choices that say you believe this is true. Diverse table fellowship is a great place to start. This is what Jesus did. When the love of Jesus is embodied in the new way by his people, love is conspicuous and peculiar. It stands out from the crowd. This is what Israel was meant to be and do, and still is, through the new Israel of the church. Be separate by the conspicuousness of your love for one another, even strangers and stragglers. Be hospitable and outward-bound with your care and affection. There is no community without demonstrable love. Put yourself in the way of it—bump into it—get some on you—be it.

8. *Emphasize quality over quantity.* Quantity is about power. It's hard to be in relationship with quantity. Quantity comes in with its chest puffed up, makes its initial impact, and then vanishes into a fog of busyness and superiority. Quality on the other hand hangs out and invites critique, meditation, and communication. Quality is not in a hurry. It gives no mind to the Dow or S&P 500. If God is concerned with quality and takes the necessary time to achieve it, so should we. He hasn't hurried in the calling of a people who would be his, in his place, under his rule.

9. *Let the Story and the new way of Jesus reinvent your understanding of wealth.* Whatever you have, be rich toward God. Invest in what he's interested in. Use your provision to continue the work of caring for his creativity. Be rich in faith, mercy, generosity, and good deeds in general. Tell a good story with the time and resources entrusted to you. They aren't yours anyway. They're on loan from God.

Whatever resources you have, keep your hope in God. Don't trust

money or power or status. There is no certainty in any of it. Avoid exces-
sive luxuries. Don't create a home you'd be ashamed to invite Jesus to.
Whatever you do, don't exploit the ignorant or the poor to create more
wealth. As far as tithing goes, forget it. In the new way, student-followers
give 100 percent. You pray, "God, everything I have is from you. How do
you want me to use it in making the kingdom visible and declaring your
rightness and excellence?"

10. Forgive as God forgave you. Have a reputation as someone who
lives a lifestyle of forgiveness. Show mercy toward people. Look at them
as if they were all dressed up in the rightness of Jesus. Imagine what they'll
look like when God gets done with them. Be quick to say you are wrong
and first to make amends. Love the unlovable. Do for others what God
has done for you.

These are my ten "first things" as I understand the new way to be
human. They inspire and support my individual role in the Story of God's
people in the world. They help me live out who and what I am, to have
human integrity and true identity. True identity is about authenticity. If I
profess to be a follower of Jesus, then I should have the same interests he
has. If I don't, my integrity is questionable.

Jesus was and is interested in love-motivated word and work. He
explained the Story, announced the kingdom, removed glaring obstacles
to health, and essentially made the rule and reign of God the King visible
in the world. In as much as God has equipped us and allowed us, we're
supposed to be about this very same business as we await the new creation. Our life is to embody God's rule and reign in the day-to-day, to
restore rightness, do justice, show mercy, and care for everything that God
loves. We are to be storytellers, telling such good stories with our lives that
they declare we belong to Jesus, the One who tells the spineless, perfect
Story. Our acceptable worship is to give up our agendas and live the certain realities of the kingdom rule and reign. Like Jesus, we invite people

to follow along. We explain the Story, announce the kingdom, and sometimes, as Saint Francis said, when necessary we use words.

~~~

I've written this book to help others navigate the ocean of life. Books accomplish this by telling good stories that make us love and respect our humanness. By good I don't mean sweet, sentimental stories untouched by the sting of life. Depending on the whole story, getting to a good outcome might be bloody and unsettling, right?

Years ago novelist Dorothy Sayers was commissioned by the BBC in the early 1940s to write a series of radio plays based on the life of Messiah Jesus. Perhaps knowing her reputation, there was some concern as to how she would depict the shocking details of the Crucifixion. In a letter to the director of the BBC, Sayers replied, "It is an ugly, tear-stained, sweat-stained, blood-stained story, and the thing was done by callous, conceited, and cruel people. Shocked? We damn well ought to be shocked. If nobody is going to be shocked, we might as well not tell them about it."

Implicitly and explicitly, good stories lead us to a better, more comprehensive vision and practice of life. It's what they do. They pull us up and into a tapestry of word and work, contentment and meaning. Some books accomplish this good by restoring a grand and beautiful hope. It's the hope of a redeemed past, a meaningful present, and a sure future. Some offer explanations and translations that turn the lights on and clear the view of obstructions. Some give just enough light so you can put one foot in front of the other. And that's enough most of the time.

I offer this book to readers as a rethinking of what is most often called the Christian life. I trust that I haven't presented a new invention or a sketchy innovation. Like a fly-fisherman carefully re-presenting his dry fly multiple times before a feeding trout, I have tried to re-present the Story, confident that the Spirit of God would instruct through it.

I'm a musician-shepherd, writing for the sheep of God's pastureland and for those who stand at the gate, ready to follow the Lamb of God through and into an excellent freedom. My mission has been to help people move from a small view of life to a comprehensive kingdom view, to help people move from what is mostly life as rote, acculturated behavior to life characterized by a full knowledge of and participation in the unfolding drama of God and his people. If any so-called Christianity or Christian theology doesn't inform, reconcile, and renew the relationship between God and people, the relationships of human persons, and the relationship between humanity and all of creation, it has not done its work. I write to invite, and the invitation is to become a serious, active participant in the Story of God-people-and-place. Hopefully the message of this book has been made abundantly clear.

In the past, taking God seriously has been associated with "sharing your faith"—the idea being that people who are serious about God are bold witnesses. Whenever and wherever, they courageously inquire as to whether a stranger knows Jesus or not. By reading this book I hope you've come to see that courage and boldness are so much bigger than this. A courageous, bold witness is not just a well-rehearsed word; it's the word-and-work witness of all God's people living out the new way to be human in the world after the pattern of Jesus. Don't settle for anything less than this. The kingdom is coming. Let your life in the now be informed by the kingdom everlasting. Dream of it, plan for it, point your compass toward obedience to what Jesus commanded. If student-followers will follow in this way, their witness would be as bold as the summer sun.

Should we ever settle for anything less than the brightest vision of who God is, who we are, and what constitutes life now and everlasting? I don't think so. In fact, it's through the living out of the reality of the kingdom that people receive the strongest word. I am not speaking against theological formulations or doctrine. I'm simply making the point that people are quicker to learn that the kingdom of God exists when it touches them, rubs off on them, and makes its presence known. When this happens, as I alluded earlier, truthful words are also good.

⌇

The story goes that a great artist was wandering the mountains of Switzerland when some officials came upon him and demanded a passport. "I do not have it with me," the artist replied. "But my name is Doré."

"Prove it," demanded the officials, knowing who Doré was, but not being certain that the wandering man was truthful.

The artist took some paper and pencil from his backpack and began to skillfully and beautifully sketch a group of peasants standing nearby.

"Enough," said the officials. "No question, you are Doré."

It is far less important for the watching world to hear you say you are following Jesus than to actually see you follow him with authenticity. All the profession in the universe is no substitute for being, knowing, thinking, and doing in the likeness of God as the Israel of God—the light of the world and the salt of the earth.

Follow Jesus. *Come and see.* Take full advantage of the new opportunity. Play an active role in the building of a new worldwide community of people who take the Word seriously and are trying to live out the new way to be human the Word teaches. Prove you are following him by the story you tell with your life. Love God and your neighbor. Care for widows and orphans. Love mercy more than being right. Tell the truth, act justly, and by all means, be humble and thankful. Never tire of doing good. Be generous and willing to share. Use whatever gift you have to serve others. Love your enemies. Hate what is evil. Do for others what God has done for you. Forgive as he forgave you. Show respect. Love the Community of Invitation. Trust God's Word. Be kind. Stay alert. Trust God for the unknown. Pray, watch, listen.

Questions for Study and Discussion

Chapter 1: Parachute Epiphanies

1. Have you ever wrestled with questions like those of the young man Charlie encountered? Explain.
2. What do you think Charlie means by "the problem of God and words is an ancient one, going all the way back to the beginning"? (See page 4.)
3. How do words and stories help you? How do they hurt you?
4. Have you ever had what Charlie calls a "parachute epiphany?" If so, describe it.
5. What do you think is meant by the phrase "a communal and storied way of knowing"? (See page 9.)
6. This chapter portrays Christians as a "multinational community that shares a defining, foundational loyalty to the Word made flesh." (See page 10.) How does this idea differ from your experience? How does it affirm it?
7. Do you see Christians as a "Community of Invitation"? Why or why not?
8. Is the Bible exhaustive knowledge of God? If not, what is it?
9. Are you sure of Jesus? Why or why not?

Chapter 2: The Jazz of God

1. What story did Jesus step into when he was born?
2. How and why do you think this question developed: "Have you accepted Jesus Christ as your personal Savior?"
3. How is telling people a Jesus story doing theology?

4. What's the difference between a Jesus story that focuses on saving people from hell and one that focuses on saving them to unceasing life with Christ?

5. What do you think it means to tell people the whole Story and invite them to participate in it?

6. In what ways do you rob the Story of its power to attract and invite?

7. Are you prepared to encounter an East Tennessee Wilderness Prophet? Why or why not?

8. What are the four main categories of the biblical Story?

Chapter 3: God, People, and Place

1. How do chapters 1 and 2 of Genesis reveal the way to be human?

2. The beginning story of God and people describes an important norm. What is it?

3. Discuss what it was like for man and woman in the beginning.

4. What is required of God's direct representative?

5. How does the idea of covenant figure into the story right from the beginning?

6. Would you say your way of being human is formed by Creational Norms? Explain.

Chapter 4: The Reality of the Fall

1. Discuss the one prohibition God gave Adam and Eve.

2. What's the connection between God's holiness and the first question the serpent asked Eve?

3. How did Satan twist the story? How was Eve a poor steward of the Word?

4. Are you ever intolerant of mystery? Explain.
5. Where does human knowing come from?
6. How did the Fall alter the relationship of God, people, and place?
7. Define and discuss sin.

CHAPTER 5: LIFE EAST OF EDEN

1. Describe and discuss life East of Eden.
2. How was Noah's call to trust God similar to that of Adam and Eve?
3. What's behind the words, Let us make a name for ourselves?
4. Is redemption as an escape from the physical world consistent with the biblical Story?
5. Discuss the promises God made to Abraham. Is this the Story you have stepped into?
6. Discuss the similarities between Noah's story and Abraham's, particularly the idea of God's using one man to save a family.
7. How did Israel understand redemption?
8. Why does God begin the prologue to the Ten Commandments with personal storytelling?
9. Discuss how the Law and covenants are a controlling, relational Story.
10. How can you better become a person of "long memory" with respect to knowing and living by the Story?

CHAPTER 6: THE OPPORTUNITY FOR A NEW WAY

1. Discuss how Jesus continued the Story begun long ago.
2. What do the cross and resurrection of Jesus mean to the Story of redemption?

3. Why is the kingdom-coming a threat to the world?

4. What is the "remarkable new opportunity" that Jesus came to invite people to participate in?

5. In light of what Jesus came announcing, discuss "church" as you know it.

6. How do students learn the new way to be human from Jesus?

7. Has the kingdom ever subverted your plans? Explain.

8. Why was the announcement of a kingdom such good news to first-century Jews?

9. How is the Story of Jesus connected to the stories of the Old Testament?

10. How is refusing to forgive someone refusing to live in the new way?

11. Discuss what repentance in the new way means.

12. What is the gift of God—the gift he wants to give?

Chapter 7: The Word and Work of Jesus

1. Jesus didn't ask Peter and Andrew if they wanted to become Christians. Discuss what he did say and the invitation he offered them.

2. Were the disciples "saved" when they first began to follow Jesus?

3. Discuss the Jesus model of Word and work, storytelling and storied living.

4. Is the Jesus way of evangelism efficient? Explain.

5. Discuss what it means to be God's direct representative today. What is the scope of such a calling?

6. When does eternal life begin?

7. What is the new identity marker for the people of God? How is this a surefire test of whether you are following in the new way to be human?

8. Learn to give a basic outline of the Story from Genesis to Jesus. Tell it to one another in everyday language.

CHAPTER 8: ONE SMALL STORY OF A LOVE SUPREME

1. How did you first step into the Story of God-people-and-place? What are your immediate family stories?
2. Are there any Christians or Christian stories in your earliest memories? Share one if you wish.
3. What is "organized religion"? Why do people often cite it as an excuse for unbelief or failure to intentionally follow Jesus?
4. How long have people been trying to get God out of the picture?
5. Why is following Jesus not self-help or a "fix"?
6. How is your experience of coming to follow Jesus similar to or different from Charlie's?
7. Discuss your understanding and practice of prayer.
8. Why is extending the invitation to follow Jesus not an option for Messiah people?

CHAPTER 9: FOLLOWING JESUS IN THE NEW WAY

1. Discuss how the new birth Jesus talked about changes a person's status in the Story of God-people-and-place.
2. In terms of brightness, how much light is in the story you are telling with your life? How does a follower of Jesus judge this?
3. Discuss the idea that your life is like an unfolding story or a piece of artwork taking shape. What do you want it to look like?
4. What does a life framed and filled with God-thoughts about reality look like? sound like?

5. What good "patterns of intentionality" would you like to focus on in this season of life?

6. What convictions do you have regarding what it means to be a human alive in God's world?

7. If you can, name a teacher who has helped you see by word and work what it means to live by God's ways?

8. How would you characterize the Jesus community in which you live out your humanness?

CHAPTER 10: THE LILY LIFE IN BEAUTIFUL VIEW, TENNESSEE

1. How are the facts, values, cares, and commitments that shape your life most evident?

2. Is it okay to put more money into something than the world says it is worth?

3. Discuss the power of place for creating and holding memories.

4. Is there such a thing as good risk? Discuss.

5. Do you trust Jesus enough to be a lily? Would you like to take him at his Word? Why or why not?

6. Charlie writes that "home can and should be an instrument of grace, an engine of truth and beauty." (See page 109.) Discuss your experience of home.

CHAPTER 11: EASTER QUIGLEY'S SLIPPERY PEARLS

1. Do you have empathy for the Easter Quigleys of the world? Did you ever put your whole heart into a relationship only to have to jerk it out again?

2. What does Charlie mean by "we don't live like the Fall is real"? (See page 115.)

3. How would you describe the difference between realism and pessimism concerning the human condition in general, and male-female relationships specifically?

4. Did you find Charlie's gender track descriptions fairly accurate? Did you take exception to them? Explain.

5. Discuss whether women were better off pre-Fall or post-Fall. If you felt women were better off in one over the other, then why?

6. How was Adam guilty at the Fall? What core stewardship role did he fail to fulfill?

7. Discuss the importance of the Word. Does God expect humans to take him at his word? Explain.

8. How is caring for God's Word essential to human work?

CHAPTER 12: RECOVERING THE STRATEGIC TEAM

1. What do you think about Charlie's idea that marriage is a strategic team assembled by God, for each other, to reveal God's excellence?

2. Discuss gender roles as you understand and practice them.

3. Discuss marital submission as found in Ephesians 5:2.

4. Discuss respect in marriage. Is it something you demand, earn, or receive? How would a man cultivate a woman's respect? How would a woman cultivate a man's respect?

5. What does it mean for you to be an imitator of God today?

6. Are you saving your life or losing it for the mission of Jesus in the world?

7. What is meant by a couple's "mutual cultural mission and mutual dignity"? (See page 127.)

8. What is God's way concerning human authority? How did Jesus model authority?

9. If you're married, how are you caring for your husband or wife? If you're single, how are you caring for your family and friends?

CHAPTER 13: KISS ME

1. Is Charlie's song "Kiss Me Like a Woman" (page 132) consistent with the Bible's view of good marriage? Why or why not?

2. If Charlie's assessment is accurate, why do you think so many Christians suffer from a lack of visible passion?

3. What does Charlie mean by "the lover's vision"? (page 136), and how does faith spark this way of seeing?

4. How do imagination and creativity play out in loving another person?

5. Discuss the role of good memory in loving each other. Discuss how some memories work against the new way to be human.

6. Are followers of Jesus free to tell the truth about their attractions and desires? What guidelines do we have to protect us against gross immodesty?

7. Are there any places of sexual hurt and damage that you are ready to talk about, ready to surrender to Jesus for his healing?

CHAPTER 14: MARRIAGE AS THE WORLD-CHANGING ART OF GOD

1. From a biblical perspective, why is sexuality always more than a private, personal thing?

2. Respond to the idea that marriage should be a "festive celebration of the Art of God." (See page 140.) What does Charlie mean by this?

3. What stories have shaped your understanding of love and marriage? How would you describe the typical controlling story for marriage that is common to your Christian communities?

4. Discuss the idea that marriage can and should change culture.

5. Discuss Brian and Kelly's understanding and practice of marriage. Were you surprised at Charlie's assessment of them? Why or why not?

6. If you are married, how would you succinctly define the controlling story behind your team of two?

7. If you are single, are you afraid of marriage in any way? Why or why not?

Chapter 15: Passionate Realism

1. Discuss the idea that there's no room for disenchantment in the new way of marriage—only passionate realism. Is this true?

2. What is consumer marriage?

3. How are you at coming clean with the stories that control you? Do you bury your wounds? Do you constantly draw attention to them?

4. What is empathy, and how is it connected to the way of Jesus?

5. Is forgiveness alive in your relationships?

6. How bad would your marriage have to get before you asked for help?

7. Why are honesty and forgiveness not only private choices?

8. Discuss how, from the very beginning, marriage has been a public way of life in the world. Still, aren't all relationships public? Discuss.

9. How would you like the next generation's ideas about marriage to change for the better?

Chapter 16: Work, Money, and the Kiss of God

1. How do you define work? What is its purpose?
2. Is caring for a flower garden work that is "inescapably connected to the Father's business in the world"? (See page 165.) If so, how?
3. Is learning the Story of God-people-and-place (and telling it to others) work? If so, what role are you playing in this stewardship work?
4. Discuss the roles of mission, motivation, and intentionality in work.
5. How is work connected to telling a good story with your life?
6. What happens when money becomes the meaning of work?
7. Are you successful? In other words, are you contributing to the building of community where a genuine ethical and spiritual life can be lived?
8. Why do we worry so much about money? What are we afraid of? How is worry not taking God's Word seriously?
9. Is this a naive idea: "Do your work and trust God to provide"?

Chapter 17: Imagination and Creativity

1. Discuss the power of imagination—the power for good and evil.
2. How do you use the word *creative?*
3. How does the ethical/moral imagination help you tell a good story with your life?
4. Define imagination. Define creativity. Discuss how they work together.
5. How are love and imagination linked in the new way to be human?
6. Are you creative? In what ways?

7. Where do we look to find norms for creative work?

8. How does the image of God within fit into the discussion of imagination and creativity?

9. Why, this side of the Fall, does Charlie say he doesn't advocate an unlimited imagination? How does he later qualify this statement?

CHAPTER 18: FAKING AND FORGETTING

1. How do we deny Jesus through our word and work?

2. Why do we want following Jesus to cost us our life? If it doesn't, what happens in its place?

3. If you are a student-follower of Jesus, is your life shaped by his identity and mission? Why or why not?

4. What is the goal of God's rescue of people and place?

5. What does Charlie mean by "Better to be weak and following the way than to have your false glory be your shame"? (See page 190.)

6. Why are faking and forgetting so dangerous?

7. How are followers of Jesus responsible for building the people of God?

8. If you are not faithful to God's agenda, what are you faithful to?

9. Would you say that your life choices reveal to your friends and neighbors that you are definitely not following the world's pattern for living?

CHAPTER 19: THE KINGDOM WAY

1. What are your thoughts about education? What kinds of education would help you better live out Jesus's Word and work agenda in the world?

2. What influence, knowledge, goods, services, and money do you steward? Take a comprehensive inventory.

3. How do you reveal God's generosity to others?

4. What does it mean for you to prepare your heart to be generous?

5. What "rubble" is Jesus urging you to breathe life into?

6. Is there anyone you can't forgive? If so, what is keeping you from forgiving?

7. What is the untold story inside of you?

8. Can you afford a crisis, a good surprise, an amazing opportunity for service?

9. Discuss Charlie's ten essential first things.

10. What does "sharing your faith" mean to you?

Whatever is true, whatever is noble, whatever is right, whatever is pure, whatever is lovely, whatever is admirable—if anything is excellent or praiseworthy—think about such things. (Philippians 4:8)

Notes

CHAPTER 1

1. Rodney Clapp, *Border Crossings: Christian Trespasses on Popular Culture and Public Affairs* (Grand Rapids: Baker, Brazos Press, 2000), 19.
2. Dr. David Clyde Jones, unpublished notes for the course formerly known as "Inspiration and Interpretation," Covenant Theological Seminary, St. Louis, Missouri.

CHAPTER 2

1. Marva J. Dawn, *Is It a Lost Cause? Having the Heart of God for the Church's Children* (Grand Rapids: Eerdmans, 1997), 117.
2. Dawn, *Is It a Lost Cause?* 117.
3. Marva Dawn, "On Teaching Children About Being the Church," *MARS HILL AUDIO Journal* (May/June 1999): MHT-38.1.4.

CHAPTER 4

1. Cornelius Plantinga Jr., *Not the Way It's Supposed to Be: A Breviary of Sin* (Grand Rapids: Eerdmans, 1995), 16.

CHAPTER 5

1. Just hours before Lt. Col. Tim Collins led his Irish troops into the conflict in Iraq, he gave his soldiers encouragement and warning: "You will be shunned unless your conduct is of the highest, for your deeds will follow you down history. Iraq is steeped in history. It is the site of

the Garden of Eden, of the Great Flood, and the birth of Abraham. Tread lightly there." Speech originally appeared in *Times of London* commentary, 23 March 2003, quoted in Lt. Col. Tim Collins, "Our Business Now Is North," *Milwaukee Journal Sentinel*, 30 March 2003. Found at www.jsonline.com/news/editorials/mar03/129286.asp.

2. N. T. Wright, *Paul for Everyone: Galatians and Thessalonians* (Reading, UK: Society for Promoting Christian Knowledge, 2002), 15.

3. A synopsis of points from Christopher J. H. Wright, *Walking in the Ways of the Lord: The Ethical Authority of the Old Testament* (Downers Grove, IL: InterVarsity, 1996), 18. For a more in-depth study of this subject, please also refer to Christopher J. H. Wright, *Living As the People of God: The Relevance of Old Testament Ethics* (Leicester, UK: InterVarsity, 1983).

4. Wright, *Walking in the Ways of the Lord*, 18.

CHAPTER 6

1. Dallas Willard, *The Divine Conspiracy: Rediscovering Our Hidden Life in God* (San Francisco: HarperSanFrancisco, 1998), 15.

2. David Wilcox, "Show the Way," © 1994 Irving Music (BMI). Used by permission.

3. Lesslie Newbigin, *The Gospel in a Pluralist Society* (Grand Rapids: Eerdmans, 1989), 16.

4. N. T. Wright, *The Challenge of Jesus: Rediscovering Who Jesus Was and Is* (Downers Grove, IL: InterVarsity Press, 1999), 46.

5. Wright, *The Challenge of Jesus*, 27.

CHAPTER 8

1. For a definition of Redbones and further reading, read Don C. Marler, *Redbones of Louisiana* (Hemphill, TX: Dogwood Press, 2003). See

also http://dogwoodpress.myriad.net/dcm/redbone.html. It's interesting reading, though some Ashworths are skeptical of its accuracy. With respect to my own Louisiana Ashworths, it has shed some light on previous family mysteries.

2. R. C. Sproul, *The Holiness of God* (Wheaton, IL: Tyndale, 1985), 218.

3. Sproul, *The Holiness of God*, 218.

CHAPTER 9

1. Steven Garber, *The Fabric of Faithfulness: Weaving Together Belief and Behavior During the University Years* (Downers Grove, IL: Inter-Varsity, 1997).

2. Inspired by Steven Garber's *The Fabric of Faithfulness*.

CHAPTER 10

1. Robert Coles, *Dorothy Day: A Radical Devotion* (Boston: Addison-Wesley Longman, 2002).

2. Robert Haney, David Ballantine, and Jonathan Elliott, *Woodstock Handmade Houses* (New York: Ballantine, 1974), intro.

3. Haney, Ballantine, and Elliott, *Woodstock Handmade Houses*, intro.

4. Awake, an organization I helped establish, "connects the church with facts and resources about the African AIDS emergency." The vision of Awake is to motivate the Christian community to become more involved in worldwide issues of justice and mercy.

5. For more information on how to get involved with helping turn the tide of AIDS and famine in Africa, please visit the following Web sites: www.datadata.org, www.oneliferevolution.org,

www.worldvision.org, www.bloodwatermission.org, and www.african leadership.org/livinghope.html.

CHAPTER 11

1. Mary Stewart Van Leeuwen, *Gender and Grace: Love, Work and Parenting in a Changing World* (Downers Grove, IL: InterVarsity, 1990), 44.

CHAPTER 13

1. Charlie Peacock, "Kiss Me Like a Woman," © 1991 Sparrow Song (BMI). All rights administered by EMI Christian Music Publishing. Used by permission.
2. A. C. Grayling, *Life, Sex and Ideas: The Good Life Without God* (New York: Oxford University Press, 2003), 47.
3. *That Thing You Do,* directed by Tom Hanks. (Los Angeles: Twentieth Century Fox, 1996).

CHAPTER 14

1. Andi Ashworth, *Real Love for Real Life* (Colorado Springs: Shaw Books, 2002), 26-27.
2. Douglas Coupland, *Life After God* (New York: Simon & Schuster, Pocket Books, 1994), 154-55.

CHAPTER 15

1. Steve Taylor, "The Finish Line," © 1993 Soylent Tunes. Used by permission.

CHAPTER 16

1. Robert N. Bellah et al., *Habits of the Heart: Individualism and Commitment in American Life* (Berkeley, CA: University of California Press, 1985), 4.
2. Leland Ryken, *Redeeming the Time: A Christian Approach to Work and Leisure* (Grand Rapids: Baker, 1995), 257.
3. Mary Pipher, *The Shelter of Each Other: Rebuilding Our Families* (New York: Ballantine, 1997), 26.
4. John Winthrop, quoted in Bellah, *Habits of the Heart*, 29.
5. Bellah, *Habits of the Heart*, 33.
6. N. T. Wright, *The Challenge of Jesus: Rediscovering Who Jesus Was and Is* (Downers Grove, IL: InterVarsity Press, 1999), 53.
7. Wright, *The Challenge of Jesus*, 53.
8. Craig Gay, *The Way of the (Modern) World: Why It's Tempting to Live As If God Doesn't Exist* (Grand Rapids: Eerdmans, 1998), 5.

CHAPTER 17

1. David Clyde Jones, *Biblical Christian Ethics* (Grand Rapids: Baker, 1994), 16.
2. Jones, *Biblical Christian Ethics*, 16.
3. Caroline J. Simon, *The Disciplined Heart: Love, Destiny, and Imagination* (Grand Rapids: Eerdmans, 1997), 14.
4. Cheryl Forbes, *Imagination: Embracing a Theology of Wonder* (Portland: Multnomah, 1986), 18.
5. Patrick Henry, *The Ironic Christian's Companion: Finding the Marks of God's Grace in the World* (New York: Putnam, Riverhead Books, 1999).

CHAPTER 18

1. Peter L. Berger, *The Noise of Solemn Assemblies: Christian Commitment and the Religious Establishment in America* (New York: Doubleday, 1961), 10.
2. *The Matrix,* directed by Larry Wachowski and Andy Wachowski. (Burbank, CA: Warner Brothers, 1999).
3. Douglas Coupland, *Life After God* (New York: Simon & Schuster, Pocket Books, 1994), 50-51.
4. Charlie Peacock and Douglas Kaine McKelvey, "William and Maggie," © 1994 Sparrow Song/River Oaks Music Company (BMI). All rights administered by EMI Christian Music Publishing. Used by permission.

CHAPTER 19

1. Jo Kadlecek, "Writing the Vivid Essay," (workshop, Festival of Faith and Writing, Calvin College, Grand Rapids, MI, March 30–April 1, 2000).
2. Dallas Willard, *The Divine Conspiracy: Rediscovering Our Hidden Life in God* (San Francisco: HarperSanFrancisco, 1998), 236.
3. Paul Sullivan, "The Cellist of Sarajevo," *HOPE* (March 1996). For a transcript, go to www.hopemag.com.
4. Dan Wooding, "First-Person: Add Ozzy to Your Prayer List," *BP News* (26 November 2002). Also found at www.bpnews.net/bpnews.asp?Id=14749.
5. Zora Neale Hurston, *Dust Tracks on a Road* (Philadelphia: Lippincott, 1942).
6. Dallas Willard, *The Divine Conspiracy,* xv.
7. Willard, *The Divine Conspiracy,* xiv.

Acknowledgments

From the moment I received the invitation to follow Jesus in the kingdom way, I entered a new life of wrestling and wonderment, questioning and studying, frustration and elation. I've had many friends, advisors, helpers, and teachers along the way. I owe a debt of gratitude to all these thoughtful, creative people. With respect to this book and the work that has gone into it, a few people deserve public mention. I am especially grateful to the following:

To my wife, author Andi Ashworth, for her ever-present encouragement, patience, and careful love, and for making beauty a norm in the place we live and breathe and have our being.

To the band Switchfoot for their song "New Way to Be Human," a title and concept that seemed to focus the material in this book better than all others. If there were a soundtrack to this book, it would be their wonderful recording *The Beautiful Letdown.* Thank you, Jon, for honoring me with such an artful foreword.

To Dallas Willard, N. T. Wright, and Christopher J. H. Wright whose scholarship and books have been a huge help and inspiration.

To Jenna Galbreth for outstanding assistance in the early stages of this book.

To Leah Payne for able assistance to the end.

To my publisher Don Pape at WaterBrook/Shaw and his supportive team, especially my praiseworthy editor, Elisa Fryling Stanford. Thanks also to Jennifer Lonas, my production editor.

To Covenant Seminary staff and students for your friendship and support, especially Professors Doriani and Jones, whom I've borrowed from liberally.

To the Art House tribe who kindly allowed me to audition much of the material from this book in their presence. Thank you for listening and for your constructive input.

To Dr. Steven Garber for the inspiration behind chapter 9.

To Al Andrews, Dr. Bruce McCurdy, and Rev. Scotty Smith for reading through parts of the manuscript, offering encouragement and correction.

To my mother, Alice; my children, Molly and Mark, Sam and Meg, and my granddaughter, Bridget; my family in Yuba City, California, and Nashville, Tennessee—thank you for loving the unlovely.

To Jesus, the Artful One, the only good King—thank you for the new kingdom opportunity that is life in you, now and always.

An Excerpt from
REAL LOVE FOR REAL LIFE

In chapter 12 I talked about marriage as a strategic team serving God's agenda together. My wife and partner, Andi Ashworth has written a book titled *Real Love for Real Life.* Her book is an excellent companion to the one you hold in your hand. If you have yet to read *Real Love for Real Life,* please enjoy a taste of it in the excerpt below:

THE SHAPE OF LOVE

We can choose to live for the glory of God in the details of our daily lives. We can spread the fragrance of Christ to others by reaching for excellence and beauty, mirroring his care for us by caring for others sacrificially and with concern for detail. People are served in unexplainable ways when all their senses are engaged: sight, sound, touch, smell, and taste. It is the details that cause us to feel cared for, that take us back in our memories to the caregivers of our past, that encourage us to pass on the touch of God in ways that others have never experienced.

My mother-in-law told me of a time when she wanted to make something special for her aunt's birthday, a woman who had spent her life caring for others. "She always had a little sweet after dinner, and I thought, 'She never has pie.' But baking pies was not at all what I did well. Still, I kept feeling a nudge to do it, so I tried—and I made the most beautiful banana cream pie ever! When Dad and I took it over, she looked shocked at first and then the tears started falling. I said, 'What's wrong, Aunt Olie?' She answered, 'I'm eighty-two years old today, and nobody has ever made me a pie.'"

Our effort to go the extra mile affirms the dignity and value of another human being. Love is incarnated, tangible, real. Just as God's personality is displayed in his creation and his care, so our personality is seen as we express God's love through the gifts he's given us for the common good.

First John 3:16 offers us a definition of love. "This is how we know what love is: Jesus Christ laid down his life for us. And we ought to lay down our lives for our brothers." For most of us, laying down our life will not happen with one grand act. Rather, it will consist of a thousand small turnings of our will from its natural self-absorption to the self-giving ways of God.

Without a vital, living relationship to Jesus, none of us can sustain a life of artful caring for long. The human heart is riddled with selfishness. As the Holy Spirit brings us to new depths of wanting to give ourselves away for Jesus's sake, the battle of our sin nature rages inside us telling us to hold back, stay safe, and keep a tight grip on our self-interests. We repeatedly come face to face with our utter dependence on God to transform us. We are drawn again to abide in Jesus, to learn from him, and to ask for creativity and strength to lay down our life for others, one person at a time.

When we care, we reflect the artistry of God. When we express his creativity, his love, and his compassion, we draw others to him—and we ourselves come to a deeper understanding of the artists he has created us to be.

About the Author

CHARLIE PEACOCK is an award-winning recording artist, producer, songwriter, and lay theologian. He is the author of *At the Crossroads* and has contributed to several books, including *It Was Good: Making Art to the Glory of God*. Peacock's music productions include Nichole Nordeman, David Crowder Band, Switchfoot, and Sara Groves. He is the writer of such popular songs as "Every Heartbeat" (Amy Grant) and "In The Light" (dcTalk). Peacock is a sought-after speaker on a variety of topics, including music, practical discipleship, and creativity. He is a contributing editor of *CCM Magazine*.

For concert and speaking booking, contact:
Mike Snider
Third Coast Artists Agency
2021 21st Avenue South, Suite 220
Nashville, TN 37212
Phone: 615-297-2021
Fax: 615-297-2776
E-mail: mike@tcaa.biz

To contact the author directly:
PO Box 218307
Nashville, TN 37221
Phone: 615-662-5876
E-mail: arthouseamerica@bellsouth.net
Web site: www.charliepeacock.com

To contact the Art House:

In Nashville, Tennessee, we have a loose group of student-followers of Jesus who gather together to promote the kind of storytelling and storied living this book talks about. We're called the Art House. If you'd like to learn more about our ministry of hospitality, art, and biblical study, contact us at one of the listings on the previous page or visit our Web site at www.arthouseamerica.com.

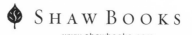

CHARLIE PEACOCK full circle
A Celebration of Songs and Friends

I'm pleased to announce that Sparrow Records has released *Full Circle,* a CD featuring new recordings of some of my best known songs. Though originally conceived as a celebration of my 20th year in Christian music, it quickly became a tribute to the relentless love and mercy of God through Jesus. Let me tell you how.

First I gathered together thirteen of my songs from the last twenty years, from "Lie Down in the Grass" (1984) to the new song "God in the World" (2004). The songs and their stories pointed me to God's faithfulness across time and the astonishing privilege of participating in His Story. For this I praised and thanked Him. Next, I recorded these songs with a cast of friends, from my earliest collaborators in Christian music, Jimmy Abegg and Mike Roe (77s), to a new friend, the wonderfully gifted songwriter, Sara Groves. This reminded me of God's careful and intricate weaving of lives, and how together as followers of Jesus, we become His word and work in the world. Again, the tribute is His: It is all the grace of God in Jesus!

I invite you to give this new recording a listen. Join me and my friends as we celebrate God's gift of music, friendship, and the Jesus way.

—Charlie Peacock

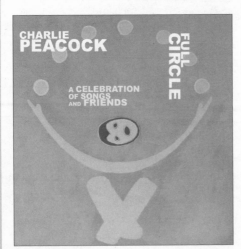

Charlie Peacock, *Full Circle: A Celebration of Songs and Friends,* released on Sparrow Records, February 24, 2004

Featuring the songs:
In the Light
Every Heartbeat
Down in the Lowlands
One Man Gets Around
Big Man's Hat, and more

Featuring the performers:
Sixpence None the Richer
Avalon
Bela Fleck
Phil Keaggy
Switchfoot
tobyMac
Out of the Grey
Darwin Hobbs
Margaret Becker
Steve Taylor
Brent Bourgeois
Bart Millard (Mercy Me)
and many others

 SHAW BOOKS
an imprint of WATERBROOK PRESS

 SPARROW®

sparrowrecords.com

charliepeacock.com